P9-CMX-242

CHICAGO PUBLIC LIBRARY

R03105 53024

	DATE DUE		

THE CHICAGO PUBLIC LIBRARY

WEST CHICAGO BRANCH
4844 W. CHICAGO AVE.
CHICAGO, IL 60651

Vaccines

Other books in the Great Medical Discoveries series:

Cloning
Gene Therapy
Tuberculosis

Great Medical Discoveries

Vaccines

by Don Nardo

Library of Congress Cataloging-in-Publication Data

Nardo, Don, 1947–
    Vaccines /Don Nardo.
        p. cm. — (Great medical discoveries)
    Includes bibliographical references and index.
    Summary: Discusses the impact of vaccines on diseases,
    their history and development, current challenges in the
    field, and future research.
    ISBN 1-56006-932-5
    1. Vaccines—Juvenile literature. [1. Vaccines.] I. Title.
    II. Series.
    QR189 .N365 2002
    615'.372—dc21

2001003198

No part of this book may be reproduced or used in any form or by any means, electrical, mechanical, or otherwise, including, but not limited to, photocopy, recording, or any information storage and retrieval system, without prior written permission from the publisher.

Copyright © 2002 by Lucent Books, Inc.
10911 Technology Place, San Diego, CA 92127
Printed in the U.S.A.

CONTENTS

FOREWORD

Throughout history, people have struggled to understand and conquer the diseases and physical ailments that plague us. Once in a while, a discovery has changed the course of medicine and sometimes, the course of history itself. The stories of these discoveries have many elements in common—accidental findings, sudden insights, human dedication, and most of all, powerful results. Many illnesses that in the past were essentially a death warrant for their sufferers are today curable or even virtually extinct. And exciting new directions in medicine promise a future in which the building blocks of human life itself—the genes—may be manipulated and altered to restore health or to prevent disease from occurring in the first place.

It has been said that an insight is simply a rearrangement of already-known facts, and as often as not, these great medical discoveries have resulted partly from a reexamination of earlier efforts in light of new knowledge. Nineteenth-century monk Gregor Mendel experimented with pea plants for years, quietly unlocking the mysteries of genetics. However, the importance of his findings went unnoticed until three separate scientists, studying cell division with a newly improved invention called a microscope, rediscovered his work decades after his death. French doctor Jean-Antoine Villemin's experiments with rabbits proved that tuberculosis was contagious, but his conclusions were politely ignored by the medical community until another doctor, Robert Koch of Germany, discovered the exact culprit—the tubercle bacillus germ—years later.

Accident, too, has played a part in some medical discoveries. Because the tuberculosis germ does not stain with dye as easily as other bacteria, Koch was able to see it only after he had let a treated slide sit far longer than he intended. An unwanted speck of mold led Englishman Alexander Fleming to recognize the bacteria-killing qualities of the penicillium fungi, ushering in the era of antibiotic "miracle drugs."

That researchers sometimes benefited from fortuitous accidents does not mean that they were bumbling amateurs who relied solely on luck. They were dedicated scientists whose work created the conditions under which such lucky events could occur; many sacrificed years of their lives to observation and experimentation. Sometimes the price they paid was higher. Rene Launnec, who invented the stethoscope to help him study the effects of tuberculosis, himself succumbed to the disease.

And humanity has benefited from these scientists' efforts. The formerly terrifying disease of smallpox has been eliminated from the face of the earth—the only case of the complete conquest of a once deadly disease. Tuberculosis, perhaps the oldest disease known to humans and certainly one of its most prolific killers, has been essentially wiped out in some parts of the world. Genetically engineered insulin is a godsend to countless diabetics who are allergic to the animal insulin that has traditionally been used to help them.

Despite such triumphs there are few unequivocal success stories in the history of great medical discoveries. New strains of tuberculosis are proving to be resistant to the antibiotics originally developed to treat them, raising the specter of a resurgence of the disease that has killed 2 billion people over the course of human history. But medical research continues on numerous fronts and will no doubt lead to still undreamed-of advancements in the future.

Each volume in the Great Medical Discoveries series tells the story of one great medical breakthrough—the first gropings for understanding, the pieces that came together and how, and the immediate and longer-term results. Part science and part social history, the series explains some of the key findings that have shaped modern medicine and relieved untold human suffering. Numerous primary and secondary source quotations enhance the text and bring to life all the drama of scientific discovery. Sidebars highlight personalities and convey personal stories. The series also discusses the future of each medical discovery—a future in which vaccines may guard against AIDS, gene therapy may eliminate cancer, and other as-yet unimagined treatments may become commonplace.

Working Toward the Goal of a Disease-Free World

When the word *hero* is mentioned, people usually envision a mighty warrior vanquishing an enemy or a firefighter rescuing children from a burning building. Though these examples of courage and ability certainly qualify as heroes, so do some scientists and doctors searching quietly and patiently, day after day, year after year, for new ways to combat disease. One of the greatest heroes of modern times was such a person. In the 1790s, a mild-mannered English country doctor named Edward Jenner discovered that he could prevent a dreaded disease by injecting patients with tiny samples of a similar but less deadly disease. He called his discovery a vaccine.

A Trail of Misery and Death

The formerly terrifying disease from which Jenner and his successors rescued millions of people was smallpox. Its characteristic symptoms and effects included severe fever, chills, pain, eruptions of pus-filled sores (pox), and very often death. For thousands of years, smallpox ravaged human communities across the world, leaving a trail of misery and death. So many people died when the disease struck ancient Rome, for instance, that there were not enough wagons to carry the dead out of the city. In desperation, the survivors threw thousands of corpses into the nearby Tiber River. Over the centuries, other outbreaks of smallpox wiped out hundreds of thousands of people a year in China, Europe, and Central America.

Fortunately, the death toll from smallpox began to decrease dramatically after Jenner developed his vaccine. In the century and a half following his discovery, many doctors in Europe, the Americas, and some other parts of the world vaccinated their patients; this simple procedure kept people exposed to the disease from becoming sick. Eventually, the governments of most developed (industrialized) countries funded programs to vaccinate most of their inhabitants.

An 1890 illustration shows children being vaccinated against smallpox.

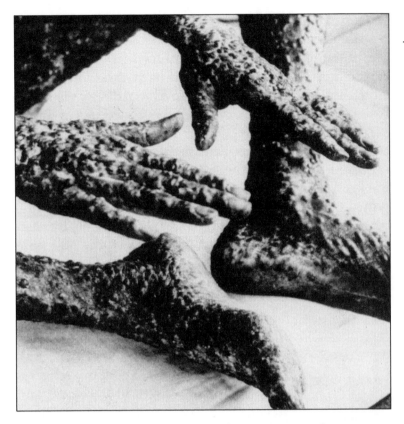

The hands, legs, and feet of a smallpox victim from the African country of Ivory Coast bear the disease's trademark sores.

In less-developed nations, by contrast, ignorance, poverty, and poor medical facilities often prevented large-scale vaccination programs. So, while well-off nations like the United States had almost eliminated smallpox by 1945, the disease continued to ravage other parts of the globe. In that year alone, for example, the government of India reported some 287,000 smallpox cases. And as late as 1967, 10 million cases of the disease, about one-fifth of them fatal, were reported worldwide.

The Concerted Eradication Effort

Disturbed by the continued suffering and high rate of death caused by smallpox, in the late 1960s the World Health Organization (WHO), an agency of the United Nations, embarked on an ambitious and unprecedented program. The goal was nothing less than the complete eradication of smallpox. WHO officials believed that, because effective smallpox vaccines were available, the disease could be beaten. What had been missing in the past, they reasoned, was concerted effort on an international scale. The agency pledged itself, therefore, to that effort and sent out hundreds of teams of doctors to vaccinate people whenever and wherever outbreaks of the illness were reported.

Under the WHO program, the eradication of smallpox occurred with astonishing swiftness. By October 1977, the last known case of the disease had been reported in Africa, and WHO proudly declared that smallpox had been eliminated from the face of the earth. This tremendous triumph of modern science remains the only case of the complete conquest of a once deadly disease.

New Generations of Vaccines

A baby receives a vaccination as part of the WHO program to eradicate smallpox.

Vaccines offer hope for eradicating other dreaded diseases besides smallpox. Over the years, scientists have developed a growing arsenal of new kinds of vaccines with such exotic names as toxoid vaccines, synthetic peptide vaccines, and recombinant vehicle vaccines. However complex their names, all work on the same basic principle demonstrated by Jenner. And all have proven effective in fighting various diseases (although none has yet succeeded in completely eliminating a disease, as the smallpox vaccine did). Vaccines have hugely reduced the incidence of polio (which causes crippling paralysis), measles, and diphtheria (which attacks the respiratory system).

In ongoing research, scientists in various countries are working to create whole new generations of vaccines to combat some of the worst scourges of humanity. Among these diseases, which together still claim millions of victims each year, are malaria, AIDS, and cancer.

The world is still far from disease free, to be sure. But a number of scientists are optimistic that the elimination of all disease, accomplished largely through various forms of Jenner's discovery—vaccines, is not an impossible goal. They are confident that the question is not, Can it be done? but rather, How long will it take?

CHAPTER 1

Fighting Disease Before Vaccines

Human existence has always been overshadowed by deadly infectious diseases. For thousands of years before the advent of vaccines, epidemics of smallpox, bubonic plague, influenza, and numerous other kinds of contagion wiped out millions of people and caused tremendous suffering and misery. Throughout most of these long ages, people did not even realize what was killing them. The germ theory—the concept that germs cause disease—was unknown until the nineteenth century. Likewise, the development and administration of life-saving vaccines did not begin until that same century.

Yet long before vaccination became a reality, people in some parts of the world recognized the basic principle behind a vaccine—using physical samples of a disease to fight a disease, thereby giving the body immunity, the ability to resist the sickness. In one way or another, members of various past cultures stumbled on and utilized this principle in treating sick people. And some of these people recovered. The problem was that no one understood *why* they had recovered. Not only did people lack knowledge of germs, they had no inkling of the complex internal physical and chemical processes by which the human body fights disease.

Ancient healers usually had to resort to a process of trial and error to find cures, therefore. Sometimes they discovered cures by accident; those who made such discoveries told others about it, spreading the knowledge to neighboring villages and eventually to other lands. In this way, ancient healers provided clues to the secrets of fighting disease, including some early understanding of the phenomenon of immunity. And though accumulated in a slow, haphazard manner, these clues eventually led researchers to the discovery and successful application of vaccines.

Smallpox in Ancient China

The most important early clues to the basic principle behind vaccination came from human experiences with

Living with Filth and Decay

The major cause of the frequent, deadly disease epidemics that ravaged humanity in past ages was the fact that people did not know that germs cause disease. Complicating this was the reality that most people lived in filthy, unsanitary conditions in which germs, both harmless and harmful, thrived. In nearly every ancient village and town, people threw their garbage into their gardens, alleyways, and sometimes even into the streets. They also disposed of human and animal wastes by dumping them into street gutters, backyard manure piles, ponds, and streams. Often, the sun dried the manure into a powder, which the wind blew over villages and houses and into open windows.

Most people were also relatively careless about the food they ate. They frequently used dirty knives to slaughter animals, then stored the meat in hot, filthy cellars that were literally breeding grounds for germs. It was also common for people to eat fruits and vegetables that insects and rodents had nibbled, and many persons did not thoroughly clean their dishes, cups, and knives after eating.

Making matters worse, it was common practice in ancient and medieval times for people to touch rotting bodies with their bare hands while moving and preparing them for burial. Moreover, during epidemics people often dumped the bodies of the victims into lakes or streams, contaminating the water. In this way, disease germs traveled from the dead to the living. It is no wonder that disease wiped out so many millions of people before the discovery of germs and vaccines.

The bodies of plague victims are loaded onto a wagon in seventeenth-century England.

one particular disease—smallpox. Modern scholars
believe that the long process that eventually led to the
discovery of vaccines began in ancient China. A little
more than a thousand years ago, a few Chinese doctors
noticed some curious, seemingly contradictory facts
about various diseases. First, a person could contract
certain illnesses over and over again. The common cold
was the most obvious example. By contrast, other illnesses, smallpox being a prominent example, usually
struck a person only once and never returned.

For uncounted centuries, the Chinese doctors observed,
smallpox had ravaged whole regions of China, almost
always displaying the same symptoms. A case of the disease started with a headache. Then pains and fever set in
and burning sores covered the victim's body, throat, and
mouth. Victims suffered uncontrollable spasms and
sometimes internal bleeding. The worst form of smallpox
caused hemorrhaging (severe bleeding) behind the nose
and eyes and ended with the person spitting up blood.
No one who reached this awful stage of the disease survived.

Because people could contract smallpox several
weeks before showing any symptoms, they could and
did infect others before realizing that they themselves
had the illness. Smallpox was so common for so long in
China that no one knows how many people the disease
killed in that land. Surely many thousands of Chinese
must have perished each year, and perhaps more than a
million died each century. Modern historians estimate
that one out of four people who contracted smallpox in
ancient and medieval times died, and many who survived retained disfiguring scars and suffered from lame-
ness or blindness.

Chinese doctors observed something else about the
smallpox survivors, something they surmised, correctly
as it turned out, was very important. For some unex-
plained reason, nearly all those who lived through a
bout with the disease never caught it again. Over time,
some of these doctors also noted that people who had

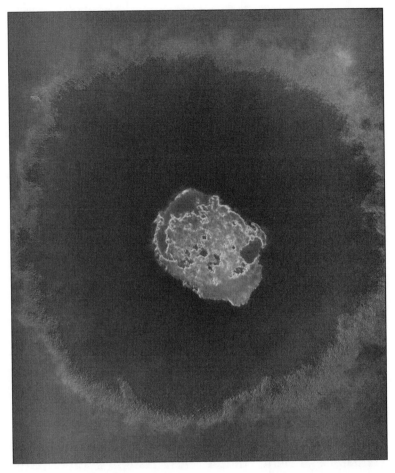

A microscopic view of the smallpox virus. Smallpox ravaged ancient China, prompting Chinese doctors to research ways to fight the disease.

suffered only mild symptoms of the disease were just as safe from later attacks as those who almost died from it. That suggested that any exposure to smallpox was enough to keep the disease from returning.

These observations became the basis for a primitive (by today's standards) but sometimes effective way of fighting smallpox. Apparently, leading Chinese doctors decided that purposely exposing people to the disease was worth the risk if it could guarantee that these persons would thereafter be safe from new attacks. So an elaborate treatment developed in which children and others who had never before had smallpox were exposed to the disease. First, doctors collected scabs from the bodies of smallpox victims who had suffered only mild symptoms. They ground up the scabs, producing a powder, which the children inhaled into their nostrils through ivory tubes. After a few days, just as expected, the children began to develop fever and smallpox sores. In most cases, however, their bouts with the illness were relatively mild. More important, the vast majority of them never again had to worry about catching this dreaded disease.

Early Inoculations

The Chinese healers who administered this often effective treatment did not know, of course, why it was successful. They did not realize that the treatment worked by strengthening their patients' immunity to smallpox. The reality is that the body can acquire immunity to a disease naturally, as in the case of a smallpox victim who survives and then remains safe from further attacks of the sickness, or artificially, as in the case of the Chinese doctors and their patients. This practice, in which a healer deliberately infects a person with a form of a disease to ward off future attacks, is called inoculation. People who are inoculated with a disease build up a tolerance for (i.e., an ability to withstand) that disease. Inoculation can also build up a person's tolerance for certain poisons.

Like the ancient Chinese, early healers in other parts of the world used these concepts without understanding how or why they actually worked. In seventeenth-century India, for example, Buddhist monks sometimes purposely swallowed small amounts of snake venom, a powerful poison. According to descriptions in several ancient writings, their intention was to make themselves immune to snakebites. Those who were successful, doctors now understand, had slowly built up a tolerance to the venom.

Some ancient African healers learned to create a similar tolerance for smallpox. Their method, passed down through untold numbers of generations of tribal healers, consisted of having healthy persons swallow smallpox scabs. A variation was to scratch a person's skin and insert fluid from a sick person's live smallpox sore. These patients, like the Chinese children who inhaled pox-infected powders, almost always contracted smallpox, but many developed only mild cases of the disease and never caught it again.

Without realizing it, all of these early healers had artificially stimulated the body's immune system. Using primitive forms of inoculation, they had helped the body strengthen its natural defenses and develop immunity against poison or disease. Nevertheless, surprisingly and for reasons that are unclear, the practice of inoculation did not become routine or widespread. Furthermore, because healers who did attempt the treatment did not understand how it worked, they sometimes mistakenly used excessive dosages and ended up killing their patients. Thus, despite the fact that some people developed immunity and survived, most of those bitten by poisonous snakes died, and epidemics of smallpox (as well as several other diseases) continued to kill thousands.

Africans, too, felt the devastating effects of smallpox. Pictured here is a statue of Sopona, a god of smallpox worshiped by the Yoruba people of Nigeria.

The Observant and Courageous Lady Montagu

Among these epidemics were several that struck Europe in the 1300s, most notoriously attacks of bubonic plague (the so-called black death) and smallpox. Smallpox struck Europe again in the centuries that followed; by the 1600s, the disease killed an estimated four hundred thousand people a year, most victims under the age of ten. This deadly onslaught continued because every new generation comprised a population who had not been exposed to the illness and therefore had no tolerance for it. Medieval European physicians, who either

A 1630 illustration depicts townspeople fleeing into the country to escape from the plague.

had never heard about or rejected the work of Chinese doctors, had no idea how to cure or prevent the disease.

In the early eighteenth century, however, thanks to a few observant and courageous individuals, Europeans began to discover important clues to the prevention of smallpox. One of these individuals was a noted English poetess, Lady Mary Wortley Montagu. In 1716 she accompanied her husband to his new post as British ambassador to Turkey. Lady Montagu herself had been badly scarred by smallpox as a child and had also lost a brother to the disease. She naturally feared losing her own children to the fever and pain of smallpox, so she was particularly intrigued by a scene she witnessed shortly after arriving in the Turkish capital of Constantinople (now Istanbul). In the company of a Turkish acquaintance, she attended a gathering of about fifteen people in a local home. There, she intently watched a primitive form of smallpox inoculation that the Turks referred to as "engrafting." Lady Montagu was unaware that this procedure was very similar to ancient Chinese and African smallpox treatments (and might, to some degree, have been copied from them).

"There is a set of old women," Lady Montagu later wrote in a letter to a friend in England, "who make it their business to perform the operation every autumn, in the month of September, when the great heat is abated [lessened]."[1]

As Lady Montagu looked on in fascination, one old woman opened a vein in a volunteer's arm. After dipping a needle into a nutshell filled with pus from small-pox sores, the old woman inserted the instrument into the open vein. She then repeated the procedure, injecting disease samples into several other veins.

Later describing the results of the treatment, Lady Montagu wrote that the patients seemed perfectly healthy for a few days. "Then," she said, "the fever begins to seize them, and they keep to their beds [for] two days, very seldom [for] three." The Englishwoman was amazed that the seemingly dangerous treatment, performed annually on thousands of Turks, was successful in most cases. In fact, a majority of patients

Lady Montagu's Remarkable Insights

Lady Mary Wortley Montagu's witnessing of a smallpox inoculation in the home of a common resident of Constantinople in 1716 was remarkable. Even male Western diplomats, like her husband, then the British ambassador to the Turkish Otto-man Empire, did not usually travel freely about the great Muslim city. But lady Montagu (1689–1762) was a determined and fearless individual. She quickly learned to speak the native language, donned the traditional clothes and veil worn by Muslim women, and explored the city, making friends wherever she went. In her later writings, she actually praised the veil, often criticized in the West as demeaning to women, as providing women with a sort of female liberation then unknown in Europe. The letters she wrote from Turkey to her friends back in England, later collected and published as the *Turkish Embassy Letters of Lady Mary Wortley Montagu*, provide fascinating insights into everyday life in Turkey, as well as political and diplomatic events, during the era.

Lady Mary Wortley Montagu observed smallpox inoculations in Constantinople.

gained permanent immunity to smallpox without serious suffering. "There is no example of anyone that had died [from] it," she wrote, "and you may believe I am very well satisfied of the safety of this experiment, since I intend to try it on my dear little son."[2]

True to her word, while living in Constantinople Lady Montagu had her son inoculated, and he survived with no ill effects. Four years later, after the Montagus had returned to London, a smallpox epidemic broke out there, and Lady Montagu realized that her daughter was at risk. In 1721, under the observation of three doctors and several newspaper reporters, Lady Montagu's daughter was inoculated. Medical authorities closely monitored and reported the young girl's progress. When she survived, inoculation as a means of controlling smallpox captured the city's attention. London was abuzz with this new notion of intentionally infecting people, particularly children, with an apparently mild case of smallpox to prevent them from coming down with a fatal or disabling case later.

Caroline of Ansbach, who would later become queen of England, ordered tests of the smallpox inoculation.

Tests on Convicts and Orphans

One Londoner who took a great deal of interest in the new treatment was Princess Caroline, the wife of the future king, George II. The princess wanted to protect her own children through the new technique, but she insisted on being absolutely sure it was safe. As an experiment, she offered freedom to six convicts who had been sentenced to die by hanging. All they had to do was to submit to smallpox inoculation; the survivors would go free. After agreeing to the deal, the six men received inoculations. Five of them contracted the disease and survived in good shape; the sixth man never became sick, probably because he had previously and unknowingly had a mild case of the disease. As she had promised, the princess freed all six men.

Princess Caroline was impressed. But she was still a bit uncertain that the technique was safe enough to use on her own children. So she ordered a group of London orphans to be inoculated. When all of them survived, just as the convicts had, she was finally satisfied that the treatment was indeed safe. She had her two daughters inoculated and they experienced no ill effects. Once the future queen of the British Empire endorsed the new technique, many ordinary British citizens followed her lead. Inoculation using samples of smallpox-infected tissue or pus spread throughout Britain and then across the English Channel to the European continent.

Inoculations in Boston

Eventually, smallpox inoculation also caught on in some of Britain's colonies, including those in North America. There, millions of Native Americans had died from smallpox during the 1500s, 1600s, and 1700s after being infected by European soldiers and colonists who had unwittingly carried the disease with them across the ocean and introduced it throughout the Americas. (Modern scholars estimate that at least 2 million, and perhaps as many as 15 million, Aztec Indians, who inhabited what is now Mexico, died of smallpox in the early 1500s alone.) European whites had managed to avoid major outbreaks of smallpox in their own communities, in part because of the practice in small cities such as Boston, in the Massachusetts colony, of isolating anyone known to be afflicted with smallpox. Inevitably, however, the disease gained a foothold. In May 1721—the same year Lady Montagu introduced inoculation to London—a smallpox epidemic erupted in Boston. While many residents panicked and fled the city, one influential clergyman, the Reverend Cotton Mather, suggested trying inoculation.

Smallpox Contributes to Spain's Victory over the Aztecs

Smallpox and other diseases brought to the Americas by European explorers and settlers killed millions of Indians in North, Central, and South America. Perhaps the worst single example of such carnage was the decimation of millions of Aztec Indians in the early 1500s. Spanish explorer-soldier Hernán Cortés landed at Vera Cruz (on Mexico's eastern coast) in 1519 and marched a small army to the great Aztec capital of Tenochtitlán (later Mexico City). Soon afterward, another Spanish force landed at Vera Cruz and the two Spanish armies eventually merged. At least one person in the second group was carrying smallpox. (The disease had crossed from Europe to the Caribbean island of Hispaniola in 1507, and by 1519 it had killed more than one-third of that island's Native American inhabitants and also spread to Cuba and Puerto Rico.) On June 30–31, 1520, the Spaniards and Aztecs fought a great battle, in which the Indians drove Cortés and his men away from Tenochtitlán. However, among the Spanish dead was the man carrying the disease. Those Indians who handled his body became infected; they soon infected others, and only a little more than a year later, millions of Aztecs were dead from smallpox, so weakening their empire that Cortés was able to defeat it easily.

Spaniard Hernán Cortés (center) easily conquered the smallpox-decimated Aztec empire.

Mather had first heard about inoculation in 1706, when he quizzed one of his African slaves about diseases the slave had suffered from before arriving in the colonies. When Mather asked about smallpox, the slave told him that he had been inoculated in Africa by a tribal healer. The man showed Mather his arm, which bore a small, circular inoculation scar. Mather recalled this incident years later when he came across an article written by Dr. Emanuel Timonius. Timonius, who had been present at the inoculation of Lady Montagu's son in Constantinople, highly recommended inoculation to fight smallpox.

During the 1721 Boston outbreak, Mather tried to interest local doctors in the idea of inoculation. But most of them were unfamiliar with the practice and skeptical of its claimed benefits. Mather then approached a physician friend, Zabdiel Boylston, with the slave's story and Timonius's article.

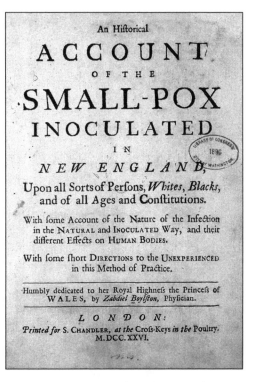

An Historical

ACCOUNT

OF THE

SMALL-POX

INOCULATED

IN

NEW ENGLAND,

Upon all Sorts of Persons, *Whites, Blacks,* and of all Ages and Constitutions.

With some Account of the Nature of the Infection in the NATURAL and INOCULATED Way, and their different Effects on HUMAN BODIES.

With some short DIRECTIONS to the UNEXPERIENCED in this Method of Practice.

Humbly dedicated to her Royal Highness the Princess of WALES, by *Zabdiel Boylston,* Physician.

LONDON:

Printed for S. CHANDLER, *at the* Cross-Keys *in the* Poultry. M.DCC.XXVI.

The title page of Zabdiel Boylston's 1726 publication describing his work with smallpox inoculation.

Boylston took immediate interest in the new treatment. In July 1721 he took scabs from some of his smallpox patients and ground them into a fine powder. Then he tested the substance on an adult slave, that slave's two-and-a-half-year-old son, and his own six-year-old son as well.

The experiment was a success. The patients whom Boylston had inoculated survived and appeared to be immune to smallpox. Mather was greatly impressed and spoke up publicly in favor of inoculation. However, a number of community leaders were alarmed that Boylston had risked further spreading the disease and afraid that inoculation might somehow backfire and kill those who submitted to it. So they outlawed the treatment in July 1721.

Defying the Ban

Soon after this prohibition, Mather's son Samuel returned home from Harvard College (in Cambridge, near Boston) with news that his roommate had contracted smallpox and died. Samuel begged his father to have him inoculated, which put the elder Mather in a desperate position. First, the technique was now illegal. Second, it was possible that if Samuel *was* inoculated, he might die from the disease. Boylston, who had continued quietly inoculating patients, had found that, although most developed only mild cases of smallpox and survived, a few had developed serious cases and died. Boylston could not explain why some inoculated people died or even predict who was most at risk.

Despite the risks, Mather decided to have Samuel inoculated, and the young man survived with no ill effects. Unfortunately, this success did not stem the unreasonable and growing fear among many Bostonians that Mather and Boylston were somehow making the epidemic worse. So when word of Samuel's inoculation leaked out, that fear exploded into violence. Someone threw a bomb through Mather's window in the middle of the night. Luckily, no one was injured, and in spite of the incident, Mather continued strongly to advocate inoculation.

A Need to Quarantine Patients

After the well-publicized inoculations in England and Boston in the 1720s, the treatment became increasingly common both in Europe and the American colonies. But inoculation was by no means foolproof in checking the spread of smallpox. In fact, people who had never been inoculated often contracted smallpox after coming into contact with those who *had* been inoculated. Because they did not know that germs caused the disease, doctors did not suspect that inoculated patients could still spread the illness to others, even before coming down with obvious symptoms themselves. The doctors did not recognize the urgent need to keep inoculated people quarantined (isolated from others) until the symptoms disappeared.

Debates over the merits and risks of inoculation continued through the second half of the eighteenth century; and those who feared the treatment often prevailed. As a result, by 1790 many towns in Europe and Britain's former colonies (which became the United States in 1776) had banned inoculation. No one dreamed that an alternative to the treatment—one that offered immunity with little or no risk of contracting disease—was possible. No one, that is, until an English country doctor conducted a simple experiment with a cow and forever changed medical science.

CHAPTER 2

The Discovery of the First Vaccines

The discovery of vaccines stands as one of the most significant breakthroughs in the history of medicine. The technique of inoculation, which works on the same principle as vaccines, had been known for centuries before Dr. Edward Jenner developed the first vaccine in the 1790s. But inoculation was a haphazard, risky treatment. Those who practiced it did not understand why it worked when it did, and sometimes it did not work. In any case, nearly everyone who was inoculated against smallpox had to endure at least a mild attack of the disease before they could acquire immunity from it.

On the other hand, Jenner's vaccine and those later developed by his medical successors offered the advantage of providing immunity to a disease with extremely low chance of contracting the disease and showing any symptoms. What made Jenner's breakthrough particularly noteworthy was that he worked without the sophisticated tools employed by modern scientists. He made his discovery with little more than natural curiosity and his own keen powers of observation and logic.

Even more remarkable, Jenner lived and worked prior to the discovery of the germ theory of disease. Eventually, thanks to French scientist Louis Pasteur and other nineteenth-century researchers, the scientific community proved the existence of germs and their connection to disease. This knowledge allowed a better understanding of how vaccines work and led to the development of increasingly more effective vaccines. Pasteur created some of these new vaccines himself and in his later years received numerous awards, as well as outpourings of heartfelt gratitude, from scientists, world leaders, and ordinary people alike.

The Mystery of the Milkmaids

Though Pasteur's predecessor, Jenner, knew nothing about germs, he knew plenty about smallpox and inoculation. As a boy of eight, in 1757, Jenner endured what he later called the worst experience of his life—a smallpox inoculation, followed by two weeks of suffering, as the symptoms of the disease wracked his young body. Luckily, Jenner lived and gained a lifelong immunity to smallpox. The experience had another, unforeseen, effect; when he grew up, Jenner became a doctor and, remembering his childhood brush with smallpox, dedicated himself to finding some way to cure this dread disease.

Because he had no idea where to start in this quest, at first Jenner employed the logical approach of collecting whatever information he could about the disease. He carefully observed and studied all aspects of the smallpox cases he treated in his own practice. And he noted the observations and anecdotes of other people who had encountered smallpox and similar diseases, including people with no medical training.

British doctor Edward Jenner devised the first smallpox vaccine.

Jenner's Inoculation Ordeal

Edward Jenner's ordeal with smallpox inoculation at the age of eight in 1757 was the result of one of the epidemics of the disease that periodically swept the British Isles. His older brother Stephen, who was also his guardian (because Edward had been orphaned at age five), ordered him to undergo the inoculation as a safeguard against catching a fatal case of smallpox. Before the procedure, Edward had to go without food for several days; then he underwent the process of bleeding, in which someone opened one of his veins and allowed some of his blood to flow into a bowl. This once-common practice was based on the false belief that human blood contained "impurities" that had to be removed for a person to maintain good health. At the time, doctors believed starving and bleeding ultimately strengthened the body, enabling it to withstand disease better.

Finally, a local druggist led Edward and some other young boys into a barn. There, the man used a knife to scratch wounds into their arms and affixed smallpox scabs to the cuts. The boys waited, in extreme hunger and discomfort, for many days; then they came down with fever, nausea, and painful sores. Weeks later, after the sores dried into scabs and fell off, the boys were allowed to leave the barn. Millions of people suffered this miserable experience in the years before the grown-up Edward Jenner discovered the first vaccine.

Indeed, Jenner was willing to follow up almost any lead, even the unsubstantiated rumor or old wives' tale. This is how he stumbled on what later came to be called the "mystery of the milkmaids." Some local farmers in Gloucestershire, the English county where Jenner lived and worked, made what seemed at the time to be an outlandish claim. The farmers said that the young girls who regularly milked their cows came down with mild symptoms of cowpox, a disease that often killed cows but was largely harmless to humans. This in itself was not unusual, since other farmworkers had been known to show temporary symptoms of cowpox. The odd part of the farmers' story was that they said these milkmaids later displayed immunity to smallpox.

Hearing this story sparked Jenner's memory of an incident that had occurred many years before when he was a young man apprenticed to a country doctor. The doctor had encountered a milkmaid who claimed she could not catch smallpox because she had already had cowpox. Dismissing her claim as pure superstition, the doctor had laughingly told Jenner, "Edward, whenever you visit your patients [once you become a doctor], take a cow with you! Wonderful animal, the cow!"[3] Once again hearing of smallpox-resistant milkmaids, Jenner began to ask his medical colleagues for their opinion. They all took the attitude of his old mentor, namely that the idea was nothing more than nonsense and superstition.

The Cowpox Inoculation Experiment

But Jenner was not so sure that his fellow doctors were right. The more he heard stories about such milkmaids, the more he came to suspect that their claims might have some basis in fact. His suspicion became even stronger in 1778 after he investigated the case of a farmer named William Smith. Smith had contracted mild symptoms of cowpox after milking his cow; Jenner noted that the cow's udders had been covered with cowpox sores at the time. Apparently, the farmer had caught the disease when pus from the sores had entered some open cuts on

The hand of the cowpox-infected Gloucestershire milkmaid from whose sores Jenner developed his inoculation.

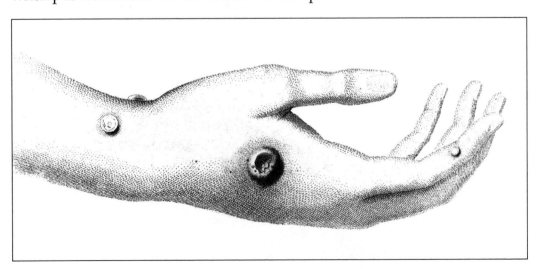

Smith's hands. This was the same manner, Jenner realized, in which smallpox entered people's bodies during inoculation. From this observation Jenner theorized that smallpox and cowpox might be different forms of the same disease, which would account for the stories of people gaining immunity to smallpox after enduring symptoms of cowpox.

This theory turned out to be incorrect. Smallpox and cowpox are two distinct diseases. Yet fortunately, the wrong guess set Jenner on the right track toward the principle of vaccination. Believing that cowpox did indeed provide immunity to smallpox, he took the next logical step. In 1796 he inoculated a healthy eight-year-old boy named James Phipps with cowpox pus. Jenner later wrote:

Jenner inoculates eight-year-old James Phipps against smallpox in 1796.

> The [cowpox pus] was taken from a sore on the hand of a dairymaid who was infected by her master's cows, and it was inserted on the 14th day of May, 1796, into the arm of a boy by means of two superficial incisions [shallow cuts] . . . each about an inch long.[4]

Seven days after the treatment, Phipps came down with minor symptoms of cowpox, including a headache and some slight chills. After a day or so, the boy was once more as healthy as ever.

Next, Jenner inoculated Phipps with pus taken from a person suffering from smallpox. The question was whether the cowpox inoculation had given the boy immunity to smallpox. When Phipps remained perfectly healthy for several weeks following the second inoculation, Jenner wrote to a friend, "I shall now pursue my experiments with redoubled ardour [passion]."[5]

Jenner had proven that inoculation with the relatively harmless cowpox could protect a person from catching the dreaded smallpox. This provided an effective and safer alternative to traditional smallpox inoculation, with a significantly higher risk of serious infection and death. To inform the European medical community of his success, in 1798 Jenner published a sixty-four-page pamphlet outlining his experiments. In the pamphlet, he called his discovery a vaccine, after the Latin name for cowpox—*Variolae vaccinae*. The word *vaccine* eventually became the universal term for any agent that provides protection against a disease by triggering the body's immune system.

Initial reaction to Jenner's findings was mixed. Some doctors thought his treatment sounded promising. Many others, though, criticized him, saying he was wasting his time trying to prove that a superstition was a fact. In the years that followed, however, physicians in England, France, and other parts of Europe repeated Jenner's experiments with the same positive results, and vaccination rapidly replaced inoculation as the preferred method for preventing smallpox. This marked the beginning of a new branch of science—immunology, devoted to the study of the body's immune system.

Success of Mass Vaccination Programs

Though Jenner at first encountered a fair amount of resistance from doctors to his smallpox vaccine, the medical community eventually accepted it. And doctors in several countries eventually convinced their governments to institute nationwide vaccination programs. The German nation of Prussia, for instance, began by vaccinating all of its soldiers in 1870 and 1871 while it was at war with France. At the time, Europe was undergoing a widespread smallpox epidemic. As the disease spread through the ranks of the armies, it became clear that the army with the most effective vaccination program would have a decided advantage. France also vaccinated its soldiers, but its program was not as widespread or efficient as that of Prussia. The result of Prussia's better program proved dramatic. During the first six months of the war, more than 280,000 French soldiers caught smallpox and 23,470 of them died. By comparison, only 8,360 Prussian soldiers caught the disease and just 297 of them died. This success encouraged Prussian officials to expand the vaccination program to the civilian population following the conclusion of the war. By 1899 Prussia had slashed its rate of death from smallpox from 4,000 people out of every million to just one person per million!

Advent of the Germ Theory

The next major breakthrough in immunology was the discovery and confirmation in the mid–nineteenth century of the germ theory of disease. This discovery finally gave scientists a clear understanding not only of the causes of many diseases, but also specifically of the way vaccines worked to make people immune from such illnesses. Scientists had known about the existence of germs for many years before Pasteur and other researchers connected them to disease. But the medical community had long assumed that these tiny agents played no major role in nature and believed them to be completely harmless.

French chemist Louis Pasteur was the first scientist who suspected these assumptions were wrong and went about proving it. In 1854, when he was thirty-two, a group of French wine makers asked him to find out what caused wine to spoil. As merchants, they hoped to reduce the incidence of spoilage and thereby save money. After conducting a number of experiments, Pasteur determined that bacteria, one of several kinds of germs then known, were the culprits in wine spoilage. This sent his brilliant mind spinning in new directions. If germs could cause wine to spoil, he wondered, might they also harm plants, animals, and people in ways that no one suspected? In fact, Pasteur became convinced that germs caused most disease.

Pasteur was right. Over the next thirty or so years, he and several colleagues confirmed the germ theory of disease. But this was not the only major contribution this remarkable man made to medical science during these years. While studying germs and disease, Pasteur also acquired an interest in finding ways to *fight* deadly diseases. He was well aware of the success of Jenner's smallpox vaccine and set out to understand how it worked and how other kinds of effective vaccines might be developed.

The Principle of Attenuation

The first vaccine Pasteur wanted to develop was for anthrax, a serious plague of sheep, cattle, and other livestock, a disease he had been studying for a number of years. But in the early stages of his research, he was interrupted by a request from a colleague, a distraction that turned out to be quite fortunate. A French veterinary scientist sent Pasteur the head of a rooster that had died of a disease known as chicken cholera. The vet believed that he had found the germ that caused the sickness, but to prove it he needed large numbers of the germs for study and experimentation. He had tried to grow a culture (a colony of several million germs), but had been unsuccessful, and so asked Pasteur for help.

Pasteur Shows How Germs Cause Spoilage

The way that Louis Pasteur discovered that germs caused wine to spoil was simple but ingenious. First, he observed samples of wine, both spoiled and unspoiled, under his microscope. He noticed large numbers of oval-shaped germs called yeasts in both batches. In the spoiled wine, in addition, he saw large numbers of smaller germs called bacteria, which had been seen many times before. The common belief was that the bacteria sprang into existence as a by-product of the process of fermentation, which changes grape juice into wine. Suddenly, Pasteur had a new idea. Perhaps the bacteria were *not* created during fermentation and maybe they were not harmless, as scientists thought. Furthermore, perhaps it was the yeasts that actually caused the fermentation process itself.

To test these assumptions, Pasteur heated mixtures of grape juice and yeasts until the yeasts had been killed. He noted that the grape juice did not change into wine. When he added yeasts to the juice, it fermented normally. This proved conclusively that yeasts caused fermentation. Pasteur now observed that as long as the wine stayed sealed, none of the bacteria entered and it did not spoil. Yet when he purposely added some of the bacteria to the wine, the liquid promptly spoiled. In this way, Pasteur showed that some germs cause fermentation, while others produce spoilage.

Nineteenth-century French chemist and bacteriologist Louis Pasteur.

Pasteur accepted the challenge, and before long found a way to grow the chicken cholera germs in culture. Pasteur placed a few of the microbes in a container of chicken broth and they rapidly multiplied to enormous numbers. Next, Pasteur and his assistants began feeding samples of the infected broth to chickens to study the various stages of the disease. The researchers immediately noticed something odd, namely that they regularly had to prepare new batches of disease-laced broth because the disease germs in a single container grew weak and died over the course of several weeks.

This observed tendency of chicken cholera germs to weaken over time led Pasteur to a accidental but important discovery. During the summer of 1879, he went on vacation and ordered his assistants to keep the germs alive during his absence by frequently transplanting them to new containers of broth. While their employer was away, however, the assistants decided to take a little vacation of their own and neglected the broth cultures. When they returned, they injected a chicken with some of the germs, fully expecting the animal to die. Instead, the animal remained alive and healthy. The

Pasteur devised a means of weakening, or attenuating, germs to provide an effective vaccine.

men realized that they had accidentally used weakened germs, so they grew a fresh, fully active germ culture and injected it into the same chicken. To their amazement, the bird still did not get sick.

The assistants could not explain why the chicken had survived. But when Pasteur returned and learned about the incident, he immediately grasped its significance. The germs from the neglected broth had been too weak to harm the chicken but strong enough to develop the bird's resistance to the disease. Because the chicken had gained immunity, Pasteur realized, the second, more harmful injection had had no effect. "Ah, this is wonderful!" the scientist exclaimed. "The secret has been found! The old culture protected the hen against the virulent [lethal] germ. Hens can be vaccinated against chicken cholera!"[6] In the next few weeks, Pasteur and his assistants repeated the experiment many times, always with the same results.

In honor of Edward Jenner, Pasteur called his new discovery a vaccine. Though similar in principle to Jenner's smallpox vaccine, however, the chicken cholera vaccine was different in one crucial respect. Jenner's vaccine was derived from a different disease than the one he was trying to prevent. Cowpox was not fatal to humans, but triggered the body's immunity to smallpox. Pasteur, on the other hand, had manipulated the very disease germ he sought to conquer. He had shown that chickens developed resistance to chicken cholera after being injected with a weakened form of the disease itself. This became known as the principle of attenuation.

Success Met with Ridicule

Pasteur reasoned that if an attenuated, or weakened, vaccine triggered immunity in birds, the same principle should hold true for other animals, including humans. Armed with this new and potent knowledge, he enthusiastically resumed his quest for an anthrax vaccine. The need for such a vaccine was certainly urgent. For several years, the disease had killed between one-quarter and

Pasteur found that weakened anthrax spores gave cattle immunity to the disease.

one-half of the cattle in France each year. Moreover, before dying these unfortunate beasts had to endure such symptoms as shaking limbs, bleeding from the mouth, and severe convulsions.

To study and experiment with anthrax properly, Pasteur and his assistants grew large numbers of cultures of the disease. Then they heated a solution containing anthrax spores—immature anthrax germs that are activated under the right conditions to grow into adult anthrax bacteria. Pasteur found that moderate heat weakened the spores and that higher temperatures killed them. Because he wanted to weaken them so that they could be used in a vaccine, he exposed some of the spore samples several times to moderate heat. When he tested the weakened germs on laboratory animals, the results were dramatic. The vaccine successfully made the creatures immune to anthrax.

To Pasteur's surprise, when he announced his achievement to the scientific community, most of his colleagues
expressed strong doubts; some even ridiculed the experiment. One noted French scientist, Dr. M. Rossignol, who
also happened to be the editor of a well-known medical
journal, wrote sarcastically:

> Will you have some germs? There are some everywhere!
> The germ theory [and Pasteur's work on vaccines] is the
> fashion. It reigns undisputed [among the ignorant]. It is a
> doctrine that must not even be argued, especially when its
> high priest, the learned Mister Pasteur, has pronounced
> the sacred words, *"I have spoken."*[7]

The "Miracle" at Melun

In the face of such ridicule, some of Pasteur's supporters
urged him to stage a public demonstration of the new
vaccine. Hoping to silence his critics, he agreed. The historic demonstration began on May 5, 1881, in a field at
Melun, a village south of Paris. A large crowd of people,
including skeptical scientists as well as members of the
French press, watched the first stage of the experiment.
Pasteur and his assistants divided a group of fifty sheep
into two lots of twenty-five each. The sheep in the first
lot received the new vaccine; the other sheep were left
untouched. Pasteur's critics were surprised when, after
a week, the vaccinated sheep remained perfectly healthy.
The critics were even more surprised when on May 17
Pasteur gave the animals a second dose of the vaccine
with no ill effect.

Then came the final and crucial stage of the demonstration. On May 31, 1881, Pasteur and his assistants
injected all fifty sheep with full-strength, deadly anthrax
germs. "A few days from now, all the vaccinated sheep
will be in perfect health," Pasteur confidently predicted.
"All unvaccinated ones will be dead."[8] Pasteur realized
fully that he was risking his professional reputation
with this bold public experiment. But he felt he had no
other choice; for the sake of science and humanity, he
had to prove that the vaccine worked.

While waiting for the final results of the fateful experiment, Pasteur returned to Paris, where he spent two sleepless nights. Then, on the morning of June 2, he received a telegram from his most vocal critic, Rossignol himself. "Stupendous success!"[9] the message read. Hardly able to contain his excitement, Pasteur hurried back to Melun. There, as he stepped from the train, a gigantic crowd greeted him with thunderous applause and shouts of acclaim, including "Miracle! Miracle!"[10] The reason for this enthusiastic reception was immediately apparent. Twenty-two of the unvaccinated sheep lay dead, and the other three were nearly dead, while all twenty-five of the vaccinated animals were alive and healthy. Rossignol, his face beaming, approached Pasteur; without further ado he admitted he had been wrong and apologized. Afterward, the two became good friends.

Pasteur performs his anthrax vaccination experiment in 1881. The demonstration was a success and Pasteur's vaccination was lauded as a "miracle."

The Next Challenge: Rabies

With conclusive proof that attenuated vaccines work on animals, Pasteur reasoned that the next logical step was to extend the idea to humans. He began studying hydrophobia, or rabies, a deadly disease usually passed to humans by animal bites. Victims of rabies suffered extreme thirst, choking, convulsions, and almost always death. At the time, the only known cure for the disease was immediate cauterization of the wounds—burning them with a red-hot iron—in hopes of killing the infection before it could invade the body. Unfortunately, this tremendously painful procedure was only occasionally successful.

Pasteur's work with rabies was slow and painstaking. In vain, he searched for the menacing disease germs under his microscope. Eventually, he concluded that these microbes were invisible because they were many times smaller than the bacteria he was used to dealing with. (Years later, other scientists would confirm this conclusion and name these smallest of all germs viruses.) Despite his inability to see the rabies viruses,

Pasteur (far left) experiments on a rabbit during his investigation of rabies.

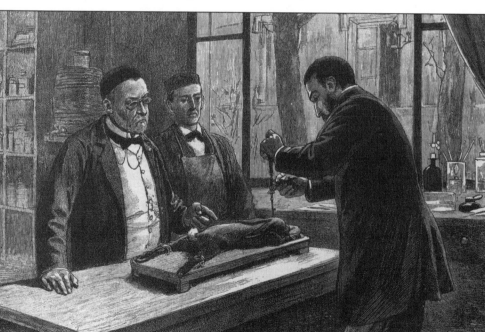

Pasteur wisely proceeded under the assumption that they did exist. He was unable to find a way to grow the germs in culture, but he discovered that he could produce a constant supply of cases of the disease for study by continually infecting successive generations of laboratory rabbits.

After more than four years of experimentation, Pasteur succeeded in attenuating rabies by drying out the spinal cords of rabbits that had died of the illness. (Rabies was known to be a disease of the nervous system, so it seemed logical that spinal cord tissue would contain high concentrations of rabies germs.) Spinal cords that had been dried for one day, he found, contained germs that were still deadly. However, cords dried for fourteen days yielded weakened, harmless rabies germs. Pasteur injected test dogs with several doses of rabies, beginning with the most attenuated germs and graduating to the more deadly ones. During this series of vaccinations, the dogs gained increased resistance to rabies until they were immune to it. Pasteur repeated the experiment on 125 dogs; all of them eventually received injections of full-strength rabies, and none of them contracted the disease.

A Life-or-Death Situation

By March 1885, Pasteur was nearly ready to try the vaccine on a human being. And he considered testing it on himself. In a letter to a friend, he wrote:

> I have not yet dared to treat human beings after bites from rabid dogs. But the time is not far off, and I am much inclined to begin by myself—inoculating myself with rabies, and then arresting the consequences [stopping the onset of the disease], for I am beginning to feel very sure of my results. [11]

A few months later, on July 6, Pasteur encountered an unexpected life-or-death situation that eliminated the need for his testing the vaccine on himself. A nine-year-old boy named Joseph Meister, accompanied by his mother, appeared in Pasteur's laboratory. Two days earlier, the boy had been bitten at least fourteen times by a rabid dog. A doctor had cauterized the wounds, but some were very deep and he doubted that young Joseph would live. Having heard about Pasteur's recent success in vaccinating dogs against rabies, the doctor urged Mrs. Meister to rush her son to Paris. If anyone could save the boy, said the doctor, it would be Pasteur.

Pasteur wasted no time in preparing the vaccine. Because he was not a medical doctor, he could not legally treat humans, so a medical colleague, Dr. Jacques Grancher, gave the boy the initial injection. Joseph received twelve shots over the course of ten days, each dose containing stronger and more lethal germs than the last. Then, there was nothing to do but wait. If the treatment failed, the boy would come down with the disease within two to ten weeks. Pasteur was nervous but hopeful. His optimism proved well placed; several weeks passed, and then several months, and to everyone's relief, Joseph Meister remained in excellent health. With this unqualified triumph, Pasteur had shown that attenuated vaccines could be used successfully to treat infected human beings.

The Way Open for New Vaccines

Pasteur's work with germs, especially his development of attenuated vaccines, remains one of the greatest scientific achievements in history. He not only saved the French cattle and fowl industries, but also rescued most of those humans who contracted rabies from terrible suffering and almost certain death. Even more important, Pasteur's observations and discoveries opened the way for the development of new vaccines to fight several other diseases.

Pasteur was the first to admit that he owed much of his success to his predecessor Edward Jenner, whose brilliant discovery of the first vaccine laid the foundation on which Pasteur and other scientists later erected the growing edifice of modern immunology. Thus, the many new and successful vaccines created in the twen-

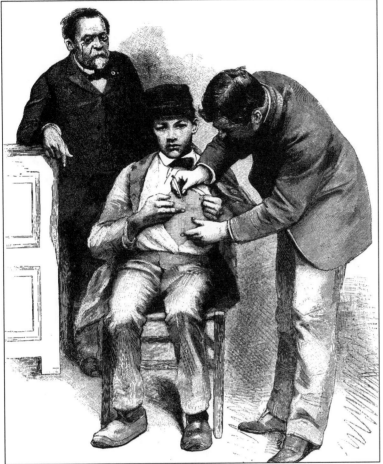

Pasteur watches as Dr. Jacques Grancher injects Joseph Meister with a rabies vaccine.

tieth century could not have become reality without the pioneering work of Jenner and Pasteur. And the hundreds of millions of people in subsequent generations who have been treated with vaccines indirectly owe their lives to these two dedicated men.

CHAPTER 3

Early Triumphs of Immunology

In the late nineteenth century and throughout most of the twentieth century, the new science of immunology enjoyed a golden age of discovery, highlighted by many dramatic breakthroughs and successes. This occurred in large part as a result of Pasteur's incredible accomplishments from the 1850s to the 1880s. He eventually completely won over those scientists skeptical of the use of vaccination for diseases other than smallpox. The days when researchers like Jenner and Pasteur had to spend much of their time defending their work were thankfully over. All members of the scientific community were now united in the belief that it might indeed be possible to eradicate many dreaded diseases.

As a result, governments and universities began encouraging and providing funds for new research. And immunology quickly expanded, as many medical researchers devoted their lives to the study of immunity and vaccines. In time, this concerted effort led to the near conquest of a number of formerly deadly diseases, among them poliomyelitis, an illness that once crippled hundreds of thousands of children each year worldwide.

Pioneers of the Post-Pasteur Era

In the immediate post-Pasteur era, scientists found that the nature and characteristics of different diseases vary a great deal. Therefore, the nature of the vaccines developed for these illnesses must also vary. Pasteur himself had suggested that attenuated vaccines might not work on every disease. His successors found that he was right and began developing alternative vaccines, including varieties called "killed" and "toxoid."

Perhaps the most important of the initial advances in immunology in the post-Pasteur era was the discovery of how the body's immune system actually works. Not even Pasteur precisely understood the functions of human cells and the body's mechanisms to fight germs and create immunity. So, ironically, as late as the mid-1880s, when millions of people were benefiting from Pasteur's vaccines, no one knew how and why these substances work.

Inspired by Pasteur, several scientists set out to explain the mechanism of immunity. Perhaps the most important

Elie Metchnikoff won the 1908 Nobel Prize in medicine for his work in immunology.

of these researchers was a Russian biologist named Elie Metchnikoff. He studied the puzzle of immunity on his own during the 1880s, then joined the staff of the Pasteur Institute in Paris. Meanwhile, working separately, German bacteriologists Paul Ehrlich and Emil von Behring performed experiments similar to those of Metchnikoff. In a relatively short time, these three men found and assembled the pieces of the immunity puzzle. By 1908 they had provided a basic picture of how the body fights disease and how vaccines create immunity. For their landmark work, Metchnikoff and Ehrlich shared the 1908 Nobel Prize in medicine. Other scientists later clarified and added detail to this explanation of immunity, especially after the invention of the electron microscope in the 1930s; this powerful magnifying device allowed scientists to study tiny germs and body cells that had previously been invisible.

How the Immune Response Works

As explained by these early pioneers, vaccines prevent disease by stimulating the body's immune response, its reaction to harmful substances that invade it from the outside. These harmful substances, most often disease-producing germs, are collectively called antigens. The body's immune response consists of the rapid production of disease-fighting cells and substances to combat and destroy invading antigens. When such an antigen enters the body and triggers the immune response, many different types of cells go to work. First, a type of white blood cell called a lymphocyte, which is produced in the bone marrow, comes into contact with and recognizes the existence of the antigen. One kind of lymphocyte, the B cell, quickly manufactures special proteins known as antibodies and releases these into the bloodstream. Another kind of lymphocyte, the T cell, does not produce antibodies, but does help stimulate the B cell to do so.

The antibodies neutralize the alien antigen in one of several ways. Some antibodies trigger chemical changes in the antigen that cause it to dissolve. Other antibodies attach themselves to and cover the antigen, rendering it incapable of reacting with and damaging the body. Still other antibodies cause chemical reactions that alter the surface of the antigen. This makes the invader stick to others of its kind, forming large antigen clumps, which usually become prey to another kind of disease-fighting cell called a macrophage. Macrophages are very large cells produced in the bone marrow, spleen, and liver. Instead of making antibodies, macrophages attack, eat, and digest an invading antigen. When an immune response begins in one part of the body, macrophages quickly travel to the site and begin devouring antigens. In these ways, all of the body's different kinds of disease-fighting cells work together to repel a foreign invader.

Natural Versus Artificial Immunity

In addition to fighting an invading disease, the cells marshaled in the immune response work to protect the body against further attacks of that disease. This is how the body builds immunity. Acquiring active immunity to disease is possible because the B cells that make antibodies have the ability to "program" themselves to a specific antigen. In other words, once an antigen of a certain disease stimulates the production of antibodies

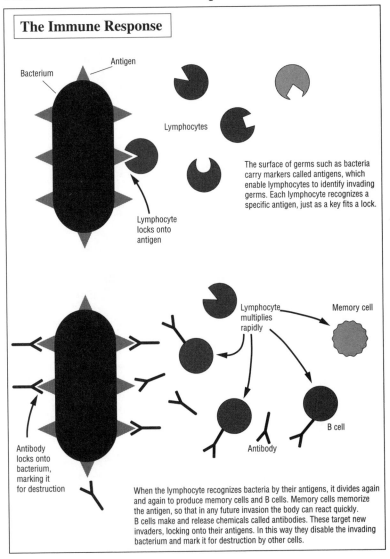

The Immune Response

Bacterium

Antigen

Lymphocytes

Lymphocyte locks onto antigen

The surface of germs such as bacteria carry markers called antigens, which enable lymphocytes to identify invading germs. Each lymphocyte recognizes a specific antigen, just as a key fits a lock.

Lymphocyte multiplies rapidly

Memory cell

B cell

Antibody

Antibody locks onto bacterium, marking it for destruction

When the lymphocyte recognizes bacteria by their antigens, it divides again and again to produce memory cells and B cells. Memory cells memorize the antigen, so that in any future invasion the body can react quickly. B cells make and release chemicals called antibodies. These target new invaders, locking onto their antigens. In this way they disable the invading bacterium and mark it for destruction by other cells.

to fight it, the B cells can later recognize another antigen of that same disease. When a person suffers a second infection of the disease, therefore, the cells of the immune system react much more quickly than they did the first time. Programmed cells also trigger an immune response to a much smaller number of antigens of the same disease. Because the second immune response is faster and stronger, it eliminates the infection before it can spread, and the person does not contract a serious case of the disease. He or she is now said to be immune to the disease.

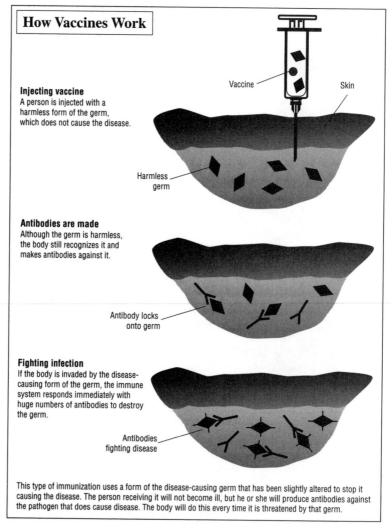

How Vaccines Work

Injecting vaccine
A person is injected with a harmless form of the germ, which does not cause the disease.

Vaccine

Skin

Harmless germ

Antibodies are made
Although the germ is harmless, the body still recognizes it and makes antibodies against it.

Antibody locks onto germ

Fighting infection
If the body is invaded by the disease-causing form of the germ, the immune system responds immediately with huge numbers of antibodies to destroy the germ.

Antibodies fighting disease

This type of immunization uses a form of the disease-causing germ that has been slightly altered to stop it causing the disease. The person receiving it will not become ill, but he or she will produce antibodies against the pathogen that does cause disease. The body will do this every time it is threatened by that germ.

However, scientists have found that the amount of time the body retains its active immunity varies from disease to disease. Immunity to some diseases—for example, yellow fever, measles, and mumps—lasts for life. In contrast, some diseases such as the common cold are caused by hundreds of similar, but slightly different, antigens; fighting off an infection of one of these antigens will not provide immunity against the others. This is why a person can catch a cold again and again.

When a person catches a disease, recovers, and develops active immunity, that immunity is said to be naturally acquired. But as Jenner correctly reasoned, a person can also develop active immunity artificially. In his case, the treatment was inoculation with cowpox, which triggered the same immune response that would have occurred if the patients had acquired the germs naturally. Pasteur used the same idea, but carried it a step further by attenuating the germs in his vaccines. These weakened germs were easily destroyed by the body's onslaught of lymphocytes and macrophages. At the same time, the weakened invaders triggered an immune response in which the body's defenses programmed themselves to fight future attacks.

Development of Killed Vaccines

As Metchnikoff and his colleagues were unveiling these basic mechanisms of the immune response, other scientists were developing new kinds of vaccines. The live attenuated vaccines developed by Pasteur had proven to be effective, and in most cases they appeared to impart long-lasting immunity. But these vaccines had one drawback. Because the germs in the vaccines were alive, a small but ever-present chance existed that a vaccinated person might actually come down with the disease and die. Immunologists now know that this occurs because a small percentage of people have impaired or weakened immune systems. Because they have trouble fighting off any kind of infection, even the weakened germs in an attenuated vaccine might be deadly to them. Other people at risk are pregnant women, whose unborn children might be infected, as well as those allergic to various substances in vaccines.

Pasteur was aware of this problem. After developing his live rabies vaccine, he performed further experiments with rabies, showing that the germs could be killed, and thereby rendered completely harmless, by treating them with chemicals. Yet for reasons Pasteur did not understand at the time, the "killed" vaccine still stimulated the development of immunity. This observation inspired other scientists to explore the possibilities of killed vaccines as a safer alternative for patients vulnerable to live versions.

In the 1880s, for example, two teams of researchers working separately developed a successful killed vaccine for hog cholera (also called swine fever). In the following years, other scientists created effective killed vaccines for human diseases, including cholera, bubonic plague, and tuberculosis. In addition, they developed other methods of killing germs, including heat and radiation.

Eventually, researchers also discovered how killed vaccines work. Although dead, the germs in such a vaccine still retain certain properties. The body's lymphocytes and macrophages have the ability to detect these properties, so the killed germs stimulate an immune response and produce immunity. But that immunity is much weaker than that created by live vaccines. Therefore, although killed vaccines are generally safer, they are not long-lasting. It is usually necessary to receive several follow-up, or booster, shots of killed vaccines to keep one's immunity active.

Toxoid Vaccines

During the development of killed vaccines, scientists discovered that germs are not the only kind of harmful antigen. In some illnesses, they found, it is secretions given off by the disease germs, not the microbes themselves, that damage the body. These poisonous secretions, called toxins, attack and kill certain body cells. Among the diseases that involve such toxic reactions are diphtheria, tetanus, and botulism.

The first disease for which researchers developed an antitoxin, or toxoid, vaccine, was diphtheria. This invader of the respiratory system causes high fever, severe congestion, nerve damage, internal bleeding, and very often death. Large diphtheria epidemics swept Europe and the United States during the nineteenth century, killing millions of people, mostly children.

As a first step, researchers injected guinea pigs with very small amounts of live diphtheria germs. This stimulated immunity in the animals without causing them to contract the disease. The guinea pigs now had in their blood specific antibodies, in this case antitoxins, programmed to fight diphtheria toxins. Next, the scientists removed fluid containing antitoxins from the blood of the immunized guinea pigs and injected it into animals that had not been immunized. When the scientists later injected the second group of animals with potent diphtheria toxin, the animals remained unharmed. The experiments proved that the antitoxins produced by the first group had stimulated immunity in the second group. After this success, scientists were able to produce toxoid vaccines in animals for use on humans. The first diphtheria vaccine appeared in 1892 and its use quickly became widespread, saving the lives of millions of people.

More advances in toxoid vaccines occurred in the twentieth century when scientists learned to deactivate disease toxins (i.e., render them harmless) by treating them with a chemical called formalin. When the deactivated toxins are injected into the body, they pose no risk of disease, just as killed vaccines offer no risk of serious infection. The deactivated toxins also stimulate an immune response that produces antibodies programmed to defend against future attacks.

The Challenge of Fighting Polio

In addition to the groundbreaking work that produced effective killed and toxoid vaccines, during the first half of the twentieth century scientists continued to develop live attenuated vaccines. This effort included vaccines to fight diseases caused by viruses, the tiniest of all germs. Perhaps the most dramatic success in this area, and without doubt one of the greatest medical achievements of all time, was the creation of an effective vaccine to prevent polio. This viral disease, more formally known as infantile paralysis or poliomyelitis, most often strikes children younger than fourteen and can cause crippling paralysis.

The huge number of children (as well as adults) struck by polio motivated scientists working in the first few decades of the twentieth century to search for an effective vaccine. In 1916 doctors reported more than 28,000 cases of polio in the United States alone, 6,000 of which resulted in death. In 1949 more than 42,000 cases were reported; and in 1952 a staggering 58,000. "There is literally no acute disease at the present day which causes so much apprehension and alarm in the patient and his relatives,"[12] wrote one prominent doctor in 1954. Echoing this concern, an article in the *Saturday Evening Post* stated, "Polio—a word that strikes more terror in the hearts of parents than the atom bomb."[13]

The fact that polio was a frightening and widespread disease was not the only driving force behind the effort

A sign encourages parents to immunize their children against diphtheria. The diphtheria vaccine was first produced in 1892.

PREVENT DIPHTHERIA
GIVE TOXOID TO YOUR CHILD
at Six and Seven Months of Age
and again on first entering school
VISIT YOUR PHYSICIAN OR A CLINIC
BALTIMORE CITY HEALTH DEPARTMENT

The Symptoms and Effects of Polio

One reason that polio was long dreaded by so many people around the world was that its symptoms and effects are particularly painful and debilitating. In a serious case of the disease, the victim first experiences pain in the back and limbs. This soon leads to partial or total paralysis, usually of the lower half of the body. The affected muscles then atrophy (become weak and useless). Sometimes the disease spreads to the respiratory or nervous systems, causing extreme difficulty in breathing, swallowing, and talking. Death can sometimes result. Because no cure yet exists for polio, victims who do not die are permanently disabled. Those with milder cases sometimes regain partial use of their limbs through physical therapy involving special exercises, but many victims are confined to beds and wheelchairs for life.

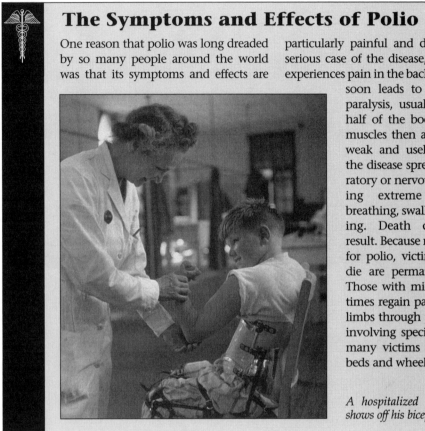

A hospitalized child with polio shows off his biceps to a doctor.

to find a vaccine to fight it. That effort could not have succeeded without a great deal of money to pay for trained researchers, laboratories, and modern medical equipment. A mass movement to raise money for polio research began when Franklin D. Roosevelt was elected president of the United States in 1932. Roosevelt had been struck by polio in 1921. He later recalled:

> When I swung out of bed, my left leg lagged. But I managed to move about to shave. I tried to persuade myself that the trouble with my leg was muscular . . . but presently, it refused to work, and then the other [leg failed].[14]

Roosevelt became permanently disabled by the disease, but through great courage and determination he

*After polio sufferer
Franklin D. Roosevelt
(center) was elected
president, money began
pouring in to fund
polio research.*

went on to become governor of New York and president of the nation. His fight against polio inspired many Americans to give money each year to a fund supporting polio research. Millions of people sent dimes to the White House in the huge fund-raising campaign that became known, appropriately, as the March of Dimes. The tens of millions of dollars collected in the 1930s and 1940s in this effort were instrumental in the eventual development of the successful vaccines that defeated polio.

Early Failures and Difficulties

The early large-scale research programs seeking a safe polio vaccine were unsuccessful. The goal was to weaken the polio virus enough to make it trigger a successful immune reaction without causing the disease. About ten thousand children were injected with a preliminary live attenuated vaccine in 1935; that same year more than eleven thousand people received another similar polio vaccine developed at a different laboratory. Both versions caused a small number of patients to contract the disease and die, so both had to be withdrawn.

Other scientists studied the unsuccessful vaccines in an attempt to find out why they had failed. These studies indicated that the chemicals used to weaken the polio viruses had not affected all of the germs. Some dangerous virus remained active in the vaccines and, when injected into patients, caused the disease. Later researchers found another reason the vaccines had failed. Scientists knew relatively little about viruses at the time, and they assumed that just one kind of virus causes polio. In the 1940s, however, came the discovery that at least a hundred different polio viruses exist. These germs fall into three general physical variations, or strains. A vaccine that works with one strain often does not work with another. This partly explains why the first two polio vaccines had worked in some cases but not in others.

Because of the failure of these vaccines, many scientists feared that live attenuated polio vaccines were

Problems in Developing Viral Vaccines

The difficulty or ease of making a vaccine depends in part on the size of the germ being cultured for the vaccine. Large germs, such as the single-celled animals known as protozoa, are easy to see and study under a conventional microscope and equally easy to work with in a culture. Bacteria are another type of single-celled organism readily visible under a microscope and easy to work with because of their size. In contrast, viruses are hundreds and sometimes even thousands of times smaller than protozoa or bacteria, and therefore are much more difficult to work with. A virus is a tiny particle of genetic material capable of invading a living cell and reproducing there. Because viruses are so tiny and live inside the cells they invade, they cannot be seen with a conventional microscope. The electron microscope, developed in the 1930s, finally allowed researchers to see viruses.

Size is not the only obstacle scientists had to overcome to create vaccines to prevent viral diseases. Viruses often mutate (change) into new forms. This means that a vaccine developed with one type, or strain, of a virus may not work against a newer, mutated form of the virus. The classic example of this drawback is influenza. In such cases, vaccines work for only a short time before they are rendered ineffective by changes in the virus.

potentially dangerous. Some researchers began to consider the idea of making killed polio vaccines instead. But whether live or killed, the polio viruses were still difficult to study and impossible to grow in the laboratory. So polio vaccine research proceeded only very slowly in the 1940s.

Toward the end of that decade, however, some important strides made the situation seem a little more hopeful. In 1948 the National Foundation for Infantile Paralysis, established in the 1930s, asked a young researcher named Jonas Salk to study and classify the different strains of polio. After much painstaking work, he confirmed the existence and varied characteristics of the three major strains. Then in 1949 scientists finally found an effective way to culture viruses in the lab. With a clearer understanding of the different polio strains and the ability to grow large supplies of them, scientists now had the basic tools they needed to zero in on an effective vaccine.

Salk's Triumph

Salk's lab soon became the focus of the mammoth effort to find a polio vaccine. In 1951, aided by fifty specialists

Jonas Salk classified the many different polio viruses into three major strains.

A Way to Culture Viruses Finally Found

One of the early difficulties of finding effective vaccines to treat diseases caused by viruses was that scientists could not culture isolated viruses under laboratory conditions. For concentrated samples of viral diseases, they had to rely on the method developed by Pasteur—cycling the diseases through the bodies of successive generations of laboratory animals. In 1949, however, three scientists working at Children's Hospital in Boston, Massachusetts, succeeded in solving this problem. John F. Enders, Frederick C. Robbins, and Thomas H. Weller managed to keep tissues from monkey kidneys alive in glass dishes. They infected the tissues with polio viruses, which spread rapidly from cell to cell in the tissues. Eventually, the tissue cells died, releasing the viruses and giving the researchers concentrated samples of the germs. This made it much easier for scientists to study viral diseases and also to manufacture viral vaccines. Enders, Robbins, and Weller shared the 1954 Nobel Prize in medicine for their achievement.

in immunology, biology, and chemistry, Salk set to work, deciding that a killed vaccine offered the best chance for a safe treatment. For two years, Salk worked eighteen hours a day, often seven days a week. He described his experiments as being similar to someone inventing a new type of cake. The baker "starts with an idea and certain ingredients," he said, "and then experiments, a little more of this, a little less of that, and keeps changing things"[15] until the cake is just right.

The first steps in Salk's recipe were to grow all three major strains of polio viruses and then to kill them. He experimented with various chemicals to see which would kill the viruses but at the same time leave them with the ability to stimulate an immune response in a vaccinated subject. Salk and his assistants finally determined that a chemical called formaldehyde worked best. When they injected the killed vaccine into test monkeys, the animals produced protective antibodies against all strains of polio. By the middle of 1953, Salk had a vaccine that was effective on monkeys; the next step was to try it on humans.

Among Salk's initial human test subjects were himself and his own family. When this vaccination and other similar tests proved successful, he informed the foundation that the vaccine was ready for a larger test. The foundation recruited the necessary subjects; beginning on April 26, 1954, Salk directed a mass vaccination of more then 1.8 million children ages six to nine. Helping in the grand experiment were 20,000 doctors, 40,000 nurses, 50,000 teachers, and 200,000 adult volunteers. Newspapers called it the greatest mass test of a scientific discovery in history.

The next step in the experiment, of course, was to monitor the vaccinated children carefully and examine their reactions to the vaccine. After nearly a year of study, Dr. Thomas Francis of the University of Michigan, who led the evaluation team, made the historic announcement. The Salk vaccine was both effective and safe, Francis told a waiting world on April 12, 1955. Wasting no time, the U.S. secretary of health, education, and welfare, Oveta C. Hobby, immediately approved the vaccine for large-scale manufacture by drug companies. "It's a great day," Hobby exclaimed. "It's a wonderful day for the whole world. It's a history-making day." [16]

These words proved to be an understatement. In the following few years, while people around the world hailed Salk as a hero, mass polio vaccinations took place in many countries. These programs were just as successful as Salk's initial tests. By 1961, six years after the introduction of the vaccine, only about 500 cases of polio were reported in the United States; Canada reported a drop from 3,900 cases a year to only 84; and results in every other nation that administered the vaccine were just as spectacular.

A Second Polio Vaccine

Despite this tremendous success, Salk's vaccine did have one drawback. Like other killed vaccines, it required subsequent booster shots to maintain patients' active immunity. This complication was potentially dangerous because many people might, for one reason or another, fail to get their boosters and contract the disease. So researchers continued to search for a live attenuated polio vaccine that would offer more long-lasting immunity.

The breakthrough came under the leadership of Albert B. Sabin, of the University of Cincinnati College of Medicine. Sabin treated the live polio viruses with chemicals, as the developers of the failed vaccines of the 1930s had. But his approach was more sophisticated. His chemicals caused mutations, physical and genetic changes, in the offspring of the germs, and all of these offspring were much weaker than their parents, so they produced no harmful effects in those vaccinated.

The Sabin vaccine has three significant advantages over the Salk version. First, because the germs in the Sabin vaccine are living, they stimulate a stronger

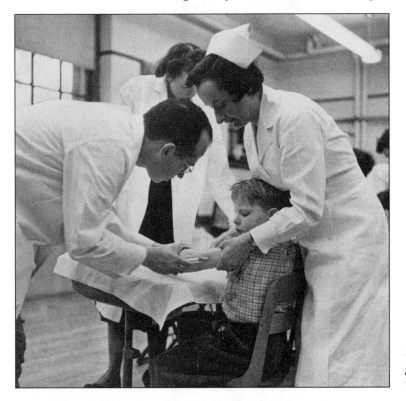

Salk injects his groundbreaking polio vaccine into a child.

immune response, which in turn imparts stronger, more long-lasting immunity. Second, once the living viruses from the vaccine are in a person's body, that person can transmit them to other people through small blood donations. So they can stimulate immunity in others, thereby extending the chain of immunized subjects. The third advantage of Sabin's vaccine is that it is easier and less painful to administer because it can be taken orally. A killed vaccine like Salk's cannot be taken orally because the digestive process would break it down and destroy its immunizing power. By contrast, living viruses like those in Sabin's vaccine can survive the trip

Albert Sabin administers his oral polio vaccine to a young girl.

through the digestive system. So doctors usually administer the Sabin vaccine in a lump of sugar or something else that tastes good.

The combined effect of the Salk and Sabin vaccines was dramatic, to say the least. By 1969 polio had nearly disappeared in the United States, Canada, Europe, and Asia. Lack of access to vaccines complicated efforts to reduce polio in Africa at first. With minor variations, though, the number of polio cases in most countries has remained very low since the 1960s.

In addition, these vaccines did more than conquer polio. Their development produced many technical advances that aided research on vaccines for other diseases. As a result, vaccine research has expanded in many directions since the 1960s, producing a number of exciting breakthroughs.

CHAPTER 4

New Horizons for Vaccines

Most of the many vaccines developed since Pasteur's time have been based on the same fundamental principles. These standard vaccines work by using either weakened or killed versions of disease-causing germs to stimulate the body's protective immunity. In the future, researchers and doctors will no doubt continue to base their work on these principles when situations warrant.

However, medical science will also utilize new types of vaccines, some of which are already in limited use or presently under development in laboratories around the world. The new techniques stem from a deeper understanding of the structure of the human body gained in the latter half of the twentieth century. In particular, modern vaccine research is based on recent discoveries about the makeup of individual body cells and the chemical processes that occur within the cells. Some researchers are focusing on the physical characteristics of disease-causing germs and the mechanisms by which these microbes trigger antibody production.

Other scientists are delving into the biological mechanisms that direct heredity, the process through which characteristics or distinguishing features pass from parents to children. These researchers have begun to manipulate such genetic mechanisms in various ways that are collectively referred to as "genetic engineering." Their goal is to use the products of these experiments to make new, more effective, and more specific vaccines.

Together, these new techniques, along with knowledge of immunology gained over the past century, will enable scientists to do many exciting things with vaccines in the twenty-first century. First, they will be able to improve the performance and reduce the risk factors of older vaccines. Second, they will develop vaccines that will work against diseases that have up to now been vaccine resistant. Advanced knowledge and technology will also allow researchers to create vaccines for diseases that are presently not well understood or that have not yet emerged to threaten humanity. Finally, vaccines may someday be used in clever ways for purposes completely unrelated to disease.

Vaccines Made from Germ Capsules

Much of the new vaccine research centers around vaccines that do not use the traditional approach of

A person getting a flu vaccine (pictured) is protected against one strain of the virus, but scientists have yet to develop effective vaccines for all types of influenza.

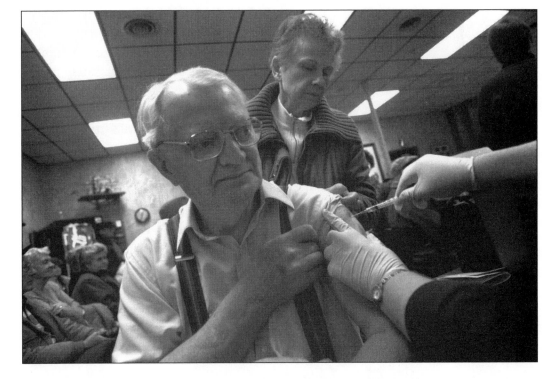

injecting whole live or killed germs into the body. The first kind of vaccine that departed from the standard approach is called a polysaccharide. Polysaccharides use just the capsules, or outer shells, that coat some germs. These capsules are composed of carbohydrates (complex sugars, hence the name polysaccharide—a combination of the terms *poly*, meaning "many," and *saccharide*, meaning "sugar"). The reasoning behind these vaccines is that the chemicals in the capsules stimulate the body's immune response and trigger the formation of protective antibodies. But because only the entire germ can cause the disease, the capsules alone are completely harmless. Therefore, if only the capsules are injected into the body, they can impart immunity without any risk of infection.

Basic research into polysaccharides began in the early decades of the twentieth century. However, not until the 1970s did laboratory technology begin to become sophisticated enough to allow significant progress in their development. The first effective polysaccharide was a vaccine for bacterial pneumonia, a severe infection of the respiratory system. The vaccine is effective against twenty-three strains of pneumonia, which cause about 90 percent of the cases of the disease in the United States each year.

Still, the vaccine is rarely used because most people who contract this kind of pneumonia can be treated effectively with the antibiotic drug penicillin. There is at present no need for large-scale preventative vaccinations. Most commonly, the doctors use the pneumonia vaccine on people who have a particularly high risk of catching the disease.

Researchers around the world continue to study polysaccharides; among the vaccines of this type presently under development are those for various kinds of influenza, often referred to simply as the "flu." Polysaccharides also hold promise for treating severe ear infections in children.

The Pressing Need for Influenza Vaccines

The potential of DNA vaccines and other kinds of innovative vaccines for preventing influenza is tantalizing to modern researchers. Influenza, usually called the "flu" for short, actually consists of numerous different strains of viruses. A vaccine that prevents one may not prevent the others; that is why scientists are trying many different avenues of vaccine research to fight the disease. The development of a range of effective influenza vaccines will come not a moment too soon. The disease still kills many people each year in various parts of the world, although no recent outbreaks have been as terrible as those of the early decades of the twentieth century. Between 1918 and 1919, for example, influenza killed at least 20 million people worldwide. In the United States alone, more than 550,000 people—ten times the number of Americans killed in World War I—perished of influenza. New, highly deadly strains of the disease could appear at any time, so modern vaccine researchers devote a good deal of energy and money to studying this disease.

An 1890 illustration shows a tent hospital for influenza patients.

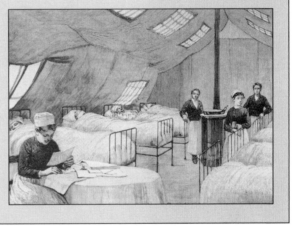

Synthetic Peptides and Malaria

Scientists are also working on other kinds of vaccines that use individual parts of germs, rather than whole germs. One of these new vaccines is called a synthetic (artificial) peptide. The strategy behind its use is to fool the body into thinking that a disease germ is invading and thus stimulate the production of antibodies. The first step in making the vaccine is to isolate the portion of the germ's surface that triggers the body's immune response. In a number of germs, this tiny piece of the organism is known as a peptide (hence the name of this variety of vaccine). Next, researchers synthesize (manufacture) an exact copy of the peptide, using various laboratory chemicals. In theory, when they inject the synthetic peptides into the body, the cells of the immune system will assume that the chemical replicas are the real thing. The cells will then mount a defense and build up immunity. And because they are artificial, they pose no risk of disease.

Many scientists believe that synthetic peptides show much promise for producing vaccines for diseases caused by protozoa. These are very large, complex germs that live as parasites inside the body. Among the many protozoan diseases are malaria, sleeping sickness, and amoebic dysentery. Of these, malaria has been targeted in the past decade by a number of researchers hoping to produce a synthetic peptide vaccine. More than 270 million people a year contract malaria worldwide, about a million of whom die. This debilitating disease causes fever, headaches, vomiting, and extreme weakness for several weeks. It can also recur without warning months or even years after the initial infection because the malaria protozoan undergoes several physical changes in the body over the course of time, each of which can trigger a new infection. Leading expert Stephen Hoffman, director

A malaria-affected woman lies on the ground of her cave home in Ta Roong, Vietnam. Malaria kills about a million people worldwide each year.

of malaria research at the Naval Medical Research Institute in Bethesda, Maryland, writes:

> Unlike measles or chicken pox, infection with malaria does not give protection against future infections because of the complex life cycle of the malaria parasite. What we have to do using modern molecular biology is something much better than mother nature can do. [17]

Other research labs are presently working diligently to find a vaccine for malaria, among them the Scripps Research Institute in San Diego, California. One of the most difficult problems to overcome, a Scripps scientist explains, is to form the artificial peptide into the shape that occurs in nature. If the shape is wrong, the immune system cells may not recognize the peptide, and the vaccine might not work. Because of this and other problems, Scripps, Naval Medical, and other labs have yet to produce a reliable malaria vaccine for humans. But the scientists involved in the research are hopeful they will be successful in the near future.

Subunit and Vehicle Vaccines

Still another type of vaccine that uses just a tiny section of a germ is the so-called subunit vaccine. What makes this version different from polysaccharides and synthetic peptides is that it applies the recently developed techniques of genetic engineering. Genetic engineers manipulate genes, tiny particles inside cells that carry coded pieces of hereditary information.

Genetic engineering developed as a result of the historic 1953 discovery by James Watson and Francis Crick of the structure of the DNA (deoxyribonucleic acid) molecule. This large, highly complex molecule, shaped like a long spiral staircase, is the principal component of the gene and specifies the genetic code that determines all of the characteristics that are passed from parents to offspring. The importance of this discovery to the science of immunology has been enormous. By studying the many links in the chain of DNA, researchers have

A model of DNA. The DNA of a disease germ can be manipulated to prevent the disease without causing the patient to contract it.

been able to isolate a specific gene in some disease germs. This gene contains "messenger" chemicals, the subunits in a subunit vaccine, that signal the body to form germ-fighting antibodies.

In the most common method of making such a vaccine, researchers separate the gene containing these chemicals from the germ. They then place the gene in a culture of harmless germs, such as baker's yeasts, where the DNA of the disease germ and the DNA of the yeasts combine and the messenger chemicals multiply. When removed from the yeasts and injected into the body, the chemicals stimulate immunity. But because the whole germ itself is not injected, the body does not contract the disease. (Because subunit vaccines are made by combining or recombining DNA from two different organisms, they are an example of an approach scientists call recombinant DNA technology.)

The first successful subunit vaccine, developed and marketed by the Merck Sharpe and Dohme pharmaceutical company, was the vaccine for hepatitis B, which the U.S. Food and Drug Administration approved for use in 1986. Hepatitis B is a serious disease of the liver and blood often contracted from infected blood during blood transfusions. The vaccine has already proved so effective that doctors in many countries are routinely giving it to infants as a preventative measure. Scientists are presently working on subunit vaccines for Lyme disease, measles, malaria, and AIDS.

Another kind of recombinant DNA vaccine under development—with the catchy name of "recombinant vehicle vaccine"—in some ways resembles a subunit vaccine. Researchers begin by separating the gene that contains the messenger chemicals from the disease germ and placing it in a harmless live germ. In the case

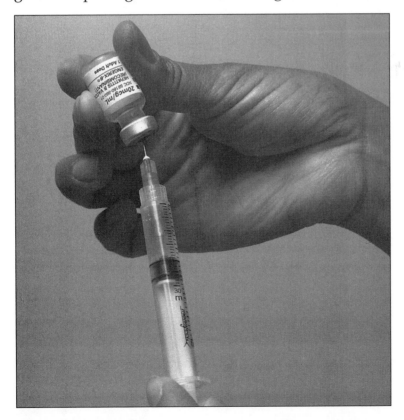

The hepatitis B vaccine (pictured) was the first successful subunit vaccine.

of a vehicle vaccine, the second germ is actually injected into the body, becoming the vehicle that carries the chemicals. These messenger chemicals then stimulate the cells of the immune system to attack the infection. Because the vehicle germs in the vaccine are harmless, like many other germs that normally live inside the body, they do not cause an infection.

The main advantage of a vehicle vaccine over a subunit version is that live germs almost always provide the strongest and longest-lasting immunity. As science writers Anna Aldovini and Richard A. Young point out: "Such vaccines should be more effective than recombinant subunit vaccines because they persist in the body for a longer period, presumably engendering [imparting] a stronger memory for the pathogen [disease antigen]."[18]

The question that most concerns researchers is, What vehicle will work best for a vehicle vaccine? Some scientists are studying cowpox, the disease Jenner used to make his smallpox vaccine, as a possible vehicle. Because the cowpox germ is relatively harmless to humans, it might safely carry the messenger chemicals of a more dangerous disease.

Researchers are also considering a type of bacteria known as BCG as a candidate for a vehicle to carry messenger chemicals. A live attenuated form of BCG has been used for many years as a safe vaccine against tuberculosis. It offers promise for carrying the messenger chemicals of another disease without posing a threat to the body. Several research labs are presently engineering BCG germs for such potential use. Scientists at these facilities have injected mice with experimental BCG vehicle vaccines for Lyme disease, tetanus, and malaria, and the mice have developed strong immune responses to these diseases. Monkeys have also been injected with a BCG vaccine for Lyme disease. Because monkeys are more closely related to humans than other animals, the results of these tests

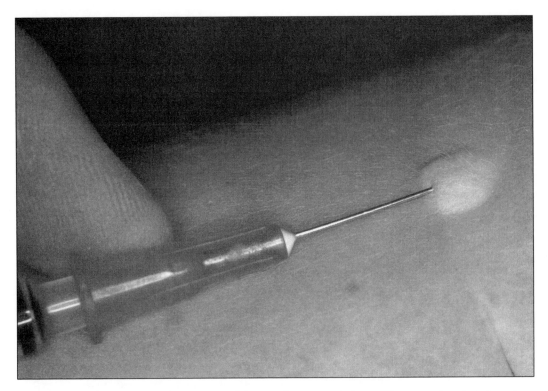

may give a better indication of how the vaccine will work on people.

A patient is injected with the tuberculosis vaccine, which uses the BCG bacteria as a vehicle.

DNA Vaccines and Edible Vaccines

An even newer and more basic way of manipulating genes to fight disease consists of taking plasmids, pieces of DNA from a harmless bacterium, and altering them genetically to resemble parts of a harmful disease germ. The altered plasmids are injected directly into human cells. Once inside a cell, some of the plasmids move into the nucleus, which responds by initiating an immune response. Although this variety of recombinant vaccine is still in the early stages of development, many researchers believe it may eventually eliminate or prevent herpes, influenza, hepatitis B, and malaria infections. Pioneering genetic researchers David B. Weiner, of the University of Pennsylvania, and Ronald C. Kennedy, of the University of Oklahoma, outline the potential benefits of DNA vaccines:

Overcoming Hurdles in DNA Vaccine Research

Although DNA vaccines show a great deal of promise, like other complex new vaccines their development presents numerous technical hurdles and problems that must be overcome before they are effective and ready for widespread use. In this excerpt from a recent article for Scientific American, *two of the world's leading experts on genetic vaccines, David B. Weiner and Ronald C. Kennedy, identify just a few of these problems.*

As the exciting, futuristic possibilities of gentic immunization are being considered, those of us who are captivated by this technology also have to roll up our sleeves and grapple with a great many details. For instance, most DNA vaccines stop yielding much protein [and thereby lose potency] after about a month. Would finding a way to extend plasmid survival lead to stronger immunity, or would it backfire and encourage attacks against unvaccinated, healthy tissue? How long does immunity last in human beings? How much do people vary in their responses? Which doses are most effective and what kinds of delivery schedules are best? We also need to know which substances are most useful for targeting genetic material to specific cells . . . and for enhancing the cellular uptake of plasmids. And which genes, out of the sometimes thousands, in a given pathogen [disease germ] should be selected for maximal power? Clinical trials answering these questions and assessing the effectiveness of the first generation of DNA vaccines may not be completed for 5 to 10 years. Whether [or not] those specific versions reach the market, though, genetic immunization technologies are likely to prove extremely valuable for research into the basic biology of the immune response and for the design of even better vaccines.

Once perfected for use in people, DNA vaccines will preserve all the positive aspects of existing vaccines, while avoiding their risks. In addition to activating . . . the immune system, they will be unable to cause infection, because they will lack the genes needed for a pathogen's replication. As a bonus, they are easy to design and to generate in large quantities using now commonplace recombinant DNA technology, and they are as stable as other vaccines (perhaps more so) when stored. They should therefore be relatively inexpensive to manufacture and to distribute widely. Further, because they can be engineered to carry genes from different strains of a pathogen, they can potentially provide immunity against several strains at once.[19]

Weiner and Kennedy stress the ease and relatively low cost of manufacturing such vaccines, factors that can ultimately determine how many people who need the vaccines will be able to afford them (or how effectively governments can mount widespread vaccination programs). Manufacturing ease and expense are also important factors motivating efforts to develop another emerging recombinant gene technology—edible vaccines. The basic approach to making such products is to combine the genetic materials of a harmful disease germ with the genes of an edible plant. The patient then ingests the altered genes during a meal (or perhaps in pill form); the body's cells then react to the presence of the germ's modified genetic materials by mounting an immune response.

Plants presently under research and development for delivery of edible vaccines include corn, potatoes, tobacco, tomatoes, bananas, lettuce, rice, and soybeans, to name only a few. The advantages of these genetically altered plants, reports a recent article in *Scientific American*,

> would be enormous. The plants could be grown locally, and cheaply, using the standard growing methods of a given region. Because many good plants can be regenerated readily, the crops could potentially be reproduced indefinitely without the growers having to purchase more seeds or plants year after year. Homegrown vaccines would also avoid the logistical and economic problems posed by having to transport traditional preparations over long distances, keeping them cold en route and at their destination. And, being edible, the vaccines would require no syringes [needles]—which, aside from costing something, can lead to infections if they become contaminated.[20]

These tomato plant leaf pieces are being used in edible vaccine research. Tomatoes may one day be used to deliver vaccines.

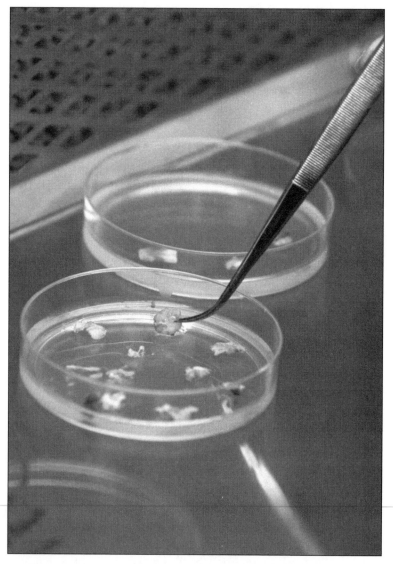

Much work is needed before safe edible vaccines that fulfill all these optimistic predictions are ready for wide-spread use. But biotechnology and pharmaceutical research companies are budgeting huge sums for drug development and it seems likely that such vaccines will become a reality eventually. As one researcher puts it, "We may some day think that getting a shot against hepatitis is a rather primitive, old-fashioned way to administer a vaccine."[21]

Pathways Beyond Imagination

If eating one's vaccines seems far-fetched now, consider that genetic engineering has also opened the door to pathways wholly unimagined by any of the early vaccine pioneers. It is unlikely that Jenner, Pasteur, or many of those who followed ever envisioned vaccines serving a purpose unrelated to preventing disease. Yet this is precisely where some vaccine research is presently leading.

Scientists in several countries are studying and testing vaccines that soon may be used to prevent pregnancy. Successful contraceptive vaccines (also called antifertility vaccines) could make women immune to pregnancy for several years at a time. Such a vaccine would trigger a woman's immune system to produce antibodies. These antibodies would bind to proteins found on the surface of men's sperm cells and destroy those cells' ability to fertilize a female egg. Early tests on female rabbits and other animals have proved successful. Injections of the vaccine stimulated their immune systems to produce antibodies to the sperm protein. Tests are also being done on baboons, and human testing is imminent.

Human tests have already taken place using a different contraceptive vaccine originally developed in Australia and India. This method prevents the implantation of the embryo in the woman's uterus *after* fertilization has occurred. It works by triggering an immune response against a hormone normally produced by the early embryo. Even if proven safe and effective, however, this type of vaccine could run into trouble in some countries. Unlike antifertility vaccines that prevent fertilization, one that prevents implantation of a fertilized egg might be viewed by some people as a form of abortion. Because abortion is highly controversial and strongly opposed by some on religious and ethical grounds, this type of vaccine may not win universal acceptance.

Nevertheless, the many technical advances and discoveries of the twentieth century—especially the manipulation of the genetic code—have opened the way for

Possible Complications of Edible Vaccines

Like DNA vaccines, edible vaccines show tremendous potential. But also like a number of other new kinds of vaccine, edible versions will still need several more years of research and refinement before they can be considered effective and safe. This critical evaluation of some of the problems involved in edible vaccine research comes from the December 2000 edition of the online journal Seedling.

Research into edible vaccines is still at a very early stage and they have a long way to go in proving their efficacy [effectiveness]. Getting plants to express [produce] adequate amounts of the vaccine is proving challenging enough, let alone translating that into an appropriate immunological response in people. Producing stable and reliable amounts of vaccines in plants is complicated by the fact that tomatoes and bananas don't come in standard sizes. There may also be side effects due to the interaction between the vaccine and the vehicle [i.e., the plant that carries the vaccine]. In many countries [especially in the developing world] . . . stringent [exacting] quality control standards for standard drugs are quite a luxury, let alone dealing with the added complications posed by edible vaccines. People could ingest too much of the vaccine, which would be toxic, or too little—which could lead to disease outbreaks among populations believed to be immune.

More research is necessary before edible vaccines are deemed safe. Here, a potato is sliced for use in one such study.

the development of a host of new and cleverly engineered vaccines in the twenty-first century. Pasteur's
dream of a vaccine for every disease may come true in
ways he could scarcely imagine. Even such dreaded
killers as AIDS and cancer may eventually be prevented
this way, as massive research efforts are presently under
way to create vaccines for these diseases.

CHAPTER 5

The Continuing Search for an AIDS Vaccine

The search for a vaccine to prevent AIDs began in the early 1980s and proceeds at an accelerated rate today. AIDS (acquired immunodeficiency syndrome) is caused by a virus known as HIV (human immunodeficiency virus), which can exist within the body for years after exposure before causing serious symptoms of AIDS. HIV is transmitted by blood and body fluids such as semen. The disease is particularly frightening because it impairs the body's immune system, leaving it open to opportunistic infection by many other diseases. At present, because no proven cure exists, AIDS is more often than not fatal, although taking certain combinations of drugs, often called "drug cocktails," has shown some promise in reducing the symptoms and extending the lives of those infected.

Another factor that makes AIDS frightening is that it is spreading rapidly, especially in the developing nations of Africa and Asia. Medical authorities at the United Nations estimate that more than 40 million people worldwide are presently infected with HIV, and that number is rising by almost 5 million a year. In the United States about forty thousand new cases of HIV are reported each year.

As alarming as the rate of infection is in the United States, it pales in comparison with the size of the AIDS problem Africa faces. In two African countries, Zimbabwe and Botswana, about 36 percent, or more than a third, of all the inhabitants are infected with HIV. And in the African nations of Namibia, Lesotho, Swaziland, South Africa, and Zambia, about 20 percent, or one in five, of the citizens are infected. The African continent as a whole holds two-thirds of the HIV-infected people in the world, which accounts for a steadily declining life expectancy in many African countries. The World Health Organization (WHO) estimates that average life expectancy in Bostwana, for example, is now forty years, compared with nearly eighty years in most developed countries.

Clearly, a cure or effective prevention method for HIV/AIDS must be found. Drug cocktails can help some of those infected live longer; but such treatment regimens are extremely expensive and are ultimately

A man with AIDS lies in a hospice outside Cape Town, South Africa. The man died the day after this picture was taken.

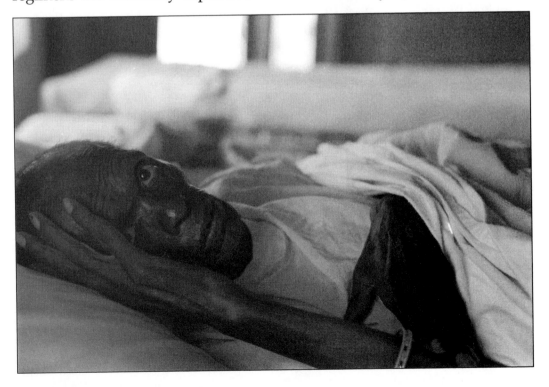

only a stopgap measure on the road to a true cure. Noted science writer Jon Cohen, who has studied the AIDS phenomenon extensively, sums up the need for a permanent method of prevention:

> Most of the world cannot afford the wonder drugs that have staved off disease and death for infected people in wealthier countries. And even in the United States, the advances celebrated a few short years ago are slipping, in no small part because the virus eventually develops resistance to every drug thrown at it. Look at AIDS deaths alone. In 1997, the year after the advent of the powerful drug cocktails, the U.S. death rate from AIDS plunged by 42%. The next year, the drop was only 20%, and the number of new AIDS cases has also nearly doubled from 1997. This is, in short, no time for any country to let down its guard against HIV, especially the United States, which spends more money on AIDS research than all other countries combined. There are many ways to slow the spread of HIV. Using condoms and clean needles, abstaining from sex, treating other sexually transmitted diseases, male circumcision, and screening blood products all have proved effective—to a point. But the best hope the world has to thwart this virus is the same weapon effectively used against smallpox, polio, hepatitis B, rabies, and other devastating viruses: a vaccine.[22]

A Host of Technical Difficulties

The search for an effective AIDS vaccine has been in progress for a full twenty years, so it is only natural to ask why the goal remains elusive. The answer is complicated because it involves a number of factors, some technical in nature, others social and financial. On the technical front, the first difficulty is that, unlike nearly all other diseases, HIV attacks the immune system itself, making a normal immune response to the disease impossible. Most normal vaccines will not work against AIDS because a vaccine imparts immunity while the body is recovering from a disease. But the body cannot recover when the immune system is not working properly. According to Aldovini and Young:

The very concept underlying vaccination, reinfection immunity, is not applicable for an infection from which there is no evidence that a person can recover. Researchers do not understand why the immune system can never rid the body of HIV . . . once it has infected a few cells. If the immune system cannot mount an effective response, scientists may not be able to design an AIDS vaccine. The major challenge to developing an AIDS vaccine may well be that HIV infects the very cells, the helper T lymphocytes [one of several kinds of T cell], that control much of the immune response. . . . And unlike the way infected cells typically respond to most invaders, a fraction of cells carrying HIV may not produce the [messenger chemicals] that alert the immune system.[23]

The other major technical problem (there are also many minor ones) in developing an AIDS vaccine is the rate at which HIV mutates into different shapes and varieties. Actually, the virus does not mutate more frequently than other disease viruses during a normal replication cycle (i.e., the time it takes for all the viruses in a given sample to replicate themselves); evidence suggests that polio viruses mutate slightly more often in any one cycle than HIV does. The problem is the blinding speed at which HIV replicates itself. A single copy of HIV can multiply about 10 billion times in a single day! Thus, HIV has more replication cycles and therefore more mutations, cumulatively, in a given time period than the viruses of other diseases.

Most of the thousands of HIV mutations are naturally defective in some way. Fortunately, these abnormal viruses cannot go on to create new strains of HIV. However, some of the mutations are *not* defective and abnormal, and these can and do generate new strains. As in the case of influenza, which also produces new virus strains all the time, researchers have trouble finding one, or even two or three, vaccines that will successfully prevent all existing strains of the disease. "The bottom line," says Cohen, "is that a vaccine made from one strain of HIV—or even say, 20 strains—may work only against a

A close-up view of HIV, the virus that causes AIDS.

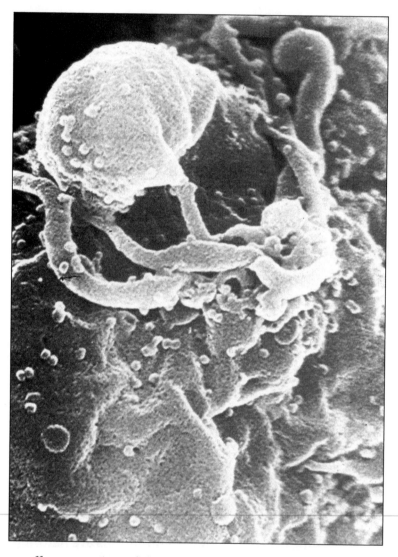

small proportion of the many extant [existing] strains of the virus now circulating in the world."[24]

Social Apathy and Lack of Funding

As for the social and financial factors that have hindered the production of an effective AIDS vaccine, the first and most damaging is negative public attitudes toward the social groups struck first and hardest by the disease. AIDS first reached public awareness in developed countries like the United States and Canada around

1980. At the time, most of its victims were male homo-
sexuals or both male and female intravenous drug users
(who frequently reuse dirty needles). The fact that
members of these groups had high rates of HIV infection had nothing to do with perceived immorality, as
some uninformed persons charged at the time. Rather,
many people in these groups unwittingly put themselves at a much higher risk of contracting HIV by prac-
ticing unprotected sex with multiple partners and using
contaminated needles. So HIV, which scientists believe
originated in Africa, naturally spread quickly among
members of these groups. (Since that time, the spread of
HIV across all sectors of the population, regardless of
sex, race, religion, income, and age, has shown that the
virus does not discriminate, as people often do.)

Nevertheless, because HIV first attacked social groups
stigmatized by large numbers of people, no collective
societal sense of urgency to find a cure emerged for a long
time. In comparison, consider the public response to
polio in the United States in the early years of the twentieth century. Polio struck more and more people each
year, a large proportion of them children. Not only did
the disease elicit a natural sympathy for the innocence of
the victims, but from the start polio struck people of all
races and creeds and sexual orientations—a true cross-
section of society. Nearly everyone knew someone or had
a connection to someone with the disease. And the president of the United States, the admired leader of the free
world, was stricken by polio. Considering all of these factors, it is not surprising that the country mounted a major
effort to combat this crippler.

By contrast, in the 1980s most Americans (as well as
most citizens of other developed countries) did not
know someone stricken with AIDS. And many felt little
or no sympathy for its victims. Once the methods of
transmission were identified in the early 1980s, a general public perception quickly emerged that as long as the
public blood supply is safely screened and one does not
engage in risky behaviors known to transmit the disease, there is very little chance of infection (which is

true). For these reasons, no widespread social sense of urgency to find an AIDS vaccine materialized.

Because of this lack of urgency, government and private funding for AIDS vaccine research took a backseat to treatment progams for those already infected. Complicating the financial situation was the fact that the big drug companies, which had the large budgets and advanced research organization needed to mount such a full-scale attack, yet initially lacked interest in developing AIDS vaccines. "Basically," Cohen explains,

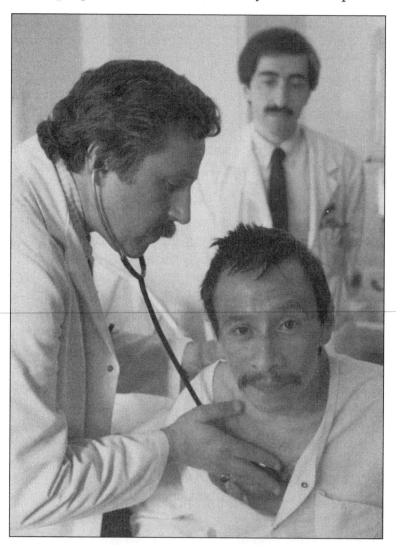

A doctor examines an AIDS patient in 1986. Since AIDS was initially not considered a threat to the general public, finding a vaccine was not a priority.

big companies deemed the risk too high. In addition to the long list of scientific unknowns, the market size [the number of potential users of the vaccine] remained a mystery, the liability issues staggered corporate attorneys [who feared that a few people who used such a vaccine would contract AIDS and then sue the company that made that vaccine for millions of dollars in damages], and developing drugs—which people need to take repeatedly for a lifetime—appeared a better financial gamble. As a result, the AIDS vaccine field mainly consisted of cash-poor biotech companies that perpetually tried to lure new investors with each tidbit of data they could produce about their "product."[25]

Trying to Set a National Goal

These factors holding back the pace of AIDS vaccine research slowly began to change during the late 1980s and through the 1990s, as the number of cases of HIV skyrocketed worldwide, increasingly among heterosexuals, non–drug users, women, and children. Evidence that a large-scale sense of urgency about developing needed vaccines was emerging at last came in 1997.

One key element that had long been missing was a strong statement of support from the highest levels of government, one that set a clear national goal and would galvanize all concerned to work toward that goal. On May 18, 1997, President Bill Clinton delivered that long-awaited statement. "Thirty-six years ago," he began,

> President Kennedy looked to the heavens and proclaimed that the flag of peace and democracy . . . must be . . . planted on the moon. He gave us a goal of reaching the moon, and we achieved it—ahead of time. Today, let us look within and step up to the challenge of our time, a challenge with consequences far more immediate for the life and death of millions around the world. AIDS will soon overtake tuberculosis and malaria as the leading infectious killer in the world. . . . So let us today set a new national goal for science in the age of biology. Today, let us commit ourselves to developing an AIDS vaccine within

the next decade. . . . It will take energy and focus and demand great effort from our greatest minds. But . . . it is no longer a question of whether we can develop an AIDS vaccine, it is simply a question of when. And it cannot come a day too soon. . . . My fellow Americans, if the 21st century is to be the century of biology, let us make an AIDS vaccine its first great triumph.[26]

This call, though certainly important as a first step, could not by itself make up for years of relative neglect by governments and drug companies and the lack of coordination among small-scale AIDS research projects. In May 1998, on the first anniversary of President Clinton's speech, the AIDS Vaccine Advocacy Coalition (AVAC) weighed in on the issue. AVAC, a private group dedicated to persuading industry and governments to work harder to create AIDS vaccines, pointed out that the full-scale mobilization the president had called for was not taking shape. "At the current level of effort," AVAC stated in a fifty-two-page report titled *Nine Years and Counting*, "we will not have an HIV vaccine in nine years."[27]

A month later, another influential private organization, the International AIDS Vaccine Initiative (IAVI) concurred with AVAC that "the world is not on track to meet the bold goal set by the U.S. President . . . to identify a safe and effective vaccine by the year 2007."[28] AVAC and IAVI had good reason for skepticism and concern. More than thirty different prospective AIDS vaccines had been developed and tested on animals (and some of them on humans) by 1998. But none had displayed any great promise of preventing the disease on a large scale. The following year, the U.S. government–funded National Institutes of Health (NIH), the largest sponsor of vaccine research in the world, funded only a single human vaccine trial; it funded none at all in the year 2000. One skeptic within the scientific community remarked, "Since it takes at least five years for a candidate vaccine to go through human trials, most scientists say that there's almost no chance they'll have a vaccine in hand by the President's 2007 deadline."[29]

Bill Clinton's Call to Arms

On May 18, 1997, at a commencement address delivered at Morgan State University in Baltimore, President Bill Clinton delivered what many people viewed as a call to arms to find an effective AIDS vacccine within ten years. In the statement, released to the media later that day by the White House press secretary, Clinton said in part:

Today, let us . . . step up to the challenge of our time, a challenge with consequences far more immediate for the life and death of millions around the world. AIDS will soon overtake tuberculosis and malaria as the leading infectious killer in the world. . . . Here at home, we are grateful that new and effective anti-HIV strategies [i.e., drug cocktails] are available and bringing longer and better lives to those who are infected, but we dare not be complacent. HIV is capable of mutating and becoming resistant to therapies, and could well become even more dangerous. Only a truly effective, preventive HIV vaccine can limit and eventually eliminate the threat of AIDS. . . . So let us today set a new national goal for science in the age of biology. Today, let us commit ourselves to developing an AIDS vaccine within the next decade. . . . There are no guarantees. It will take energy and focus and demand great effort from out greatest minds. But with the strides of recent years it is no longer a question of whether we can develop an AIDS vaccine, it is simply a question of when. And it cannot come a day too soon. If America commits to finding an AIDS

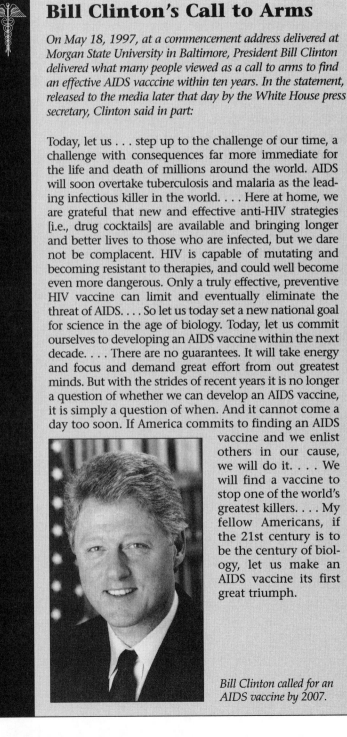

vaccine and we enlist others in our cause, we will do it. . . . We will find a vaccine to stop one of the world's greatest killers. . . . My fellow Americans, if the 21st century is to be the century of biology, let us make an AIDS vaccine its first great triumph.

Bill Clinton called for an AIDS vaccine by 2007.

New Clinical Trials in Africa

As it turns out, this pessimistic prediction may be premature. Although no massive coordinated international effort to create an AIDS vaccine has yet been mounted, some important progress has been made by independent research groups since the 1998 AVAC and IAVI reports came out. First, the IAVI itself offered to raise the funds needed to create one or more international development teams that would bring vaccine researchers, major private-sector donors, and medical experts together in a united effort, even if on a small scale. True to its word, backed by the United Nations, IAVI quickly raised enough money to create the first development team. (Among the financial contributors were the William H. Gates Foundation, World Bank, and Levi Strauss Foundation.)

The IAVI-backed team, consisting of scientists from the Human Immunology Unit (headed by renowned immunologist Andrew McMichael) at Oxford University, in England, and the University of Nairobi, in Kenya, focused its attention on Africa, since that continent has been hardest hit by the AIDS epidemic. Specifically, the team targeted the strain of the HIV virus most common in East Africa. The question, of course, was which approach to take in creating a vaccine. Researchers around the world had been and still were working on live attenuated versions, killed versions, and especially various subunit, vehicle, and DNA versions. The team did have a strong lead to pursue, though, in choosing an approach. Medical reporter Meredith Wadman explains that the approach

> grew out of an extraordinary finding in [studies of] prostitutes in Nairobi. These women have upwards of 1,000 sexual encounters a year in a city where it's estimated that more than 30% of the adult population is HIV-positive. Yet a small minority of the women remain uninfected. Researchers found no virus and no HIV antibodies in their blood. What they did find sent McMichael back to his lab: Killer T-cells were protecting the women.[30]

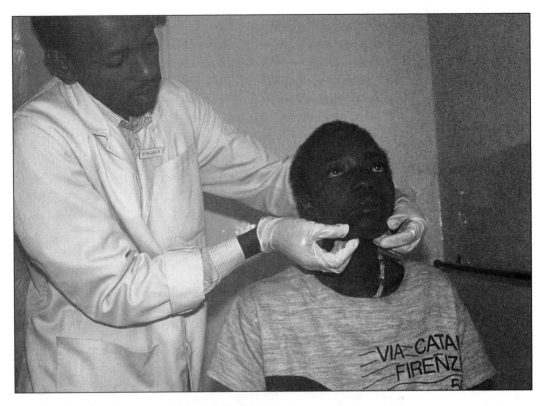

A doctor checks the lymph glands of an East African prostitute as part of an HIV study in Nairobi, Kenya.

This finding was significant because, in creating any vaccine, scientists usually aim to induce a normal immune response. In such a response, the body's helper T cells (special lymphocytes that can attack antigens or infected cells) are critical in mounting an all-out attack on invading antigens. However, these cells normally do not act alone, but rather in concert with antibodies and other defensive agents. Because the T cells alone seemed to be the active agent in protecting the prostitutes from contracting HIV, McMichael's team targeted the T cells. They engineered a DNA vaccine out of DNA strands taken from the common East African HIV strain. They designed it to enter a person's cells, reach the nucleus, and there stimulate production of T cells.

A number of scientists are skeptical, saying that a vaccine that stimulates only the production of T cells may not be potent enough to do the job. But McMichael and his colleagues optimistically began large-scale human trials of their new vaccine in Kenya in March 2001. The first person to receive this first vaccine specifically targeted for and tested on Africans was Pamela Mandela Indenye, a thirty-one-year-old surgeon. To calm fears that would deter potential volunteers from participating in the trial, one team leader explained that the vaccine contains no whole germs, either live or killed; so it is

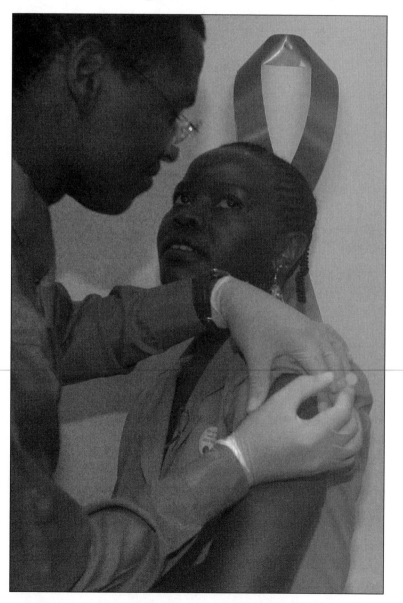

A Kenyan scientist injects volunteer Pamela Mandela Indeyne with an AIDS vaccine on March 6, 2001.

safe. "I would like to emphasize," he said, "that it is not possible to acquire HIV/AIDS as a result of using the vaccine under trial. We are not injecting the volunteers with a [whole] virus, either in its live or lifeless form."[31]

Success Now Seen as Inevitable

While the world waits for the results of the IAVI-sponsored African trials, research into AIDS vaccines continues in labs around the world. One hopeful study, conducted independently of the work of the IAVI African team, appears to support the T cell approach employed by that team. In September 2000, a group of investigators headed by Bruce Walker at Massachusetts General Hospital, in Boston, published the results of their study in the prestigious journal *Nature*. To test whether T cells alone could fight HIV infection, Walker and his colleagues gave HIV-positive patients potent antiviral drugs in the first few days or weeks after they had contracted the virus. This is the crucial, acute period during which HIV normally cripples the immune system, preventing the T cells from mounting an aggressive defense. The drugs knock HIV down to very low levels before the virus can destroy the vital helper T cells. The doctors then temporarily discontinued the antiviral drugs, and the T cells took over, controlling the levels of HIV in the patients' bloodstreams, and allowing the patients to remain symptom free without drug therapy for extended periods.

Meanwhile, a different but equally hopeful approach has emerged in Durham, North Carolina. There, at AlphaVax, a biotech company partially funded by IAVI, a recombinant vehicle vaccine is nearing the crucial stage of human trials. The vaccine, which targets an HIV strain predominant in South Africa, cleverly uses as its vehicle a virus from a disease called Venezuelan equine encephalitis (VEE). The VEE will carry the engineered genes to a person's lymph nodes, where much of the body's battle against HIV takes place. In tests on monkeys, the vaccine stimulated the production of large numbers of both T cells and antibodies and stopped the HIV infection.

In addition to these efforts, other organizations have followed IAVI's lead. The National Institute of Allergy and Infectious Diseases (NIAID), headquartered in Bethesda, Maryland, recently announced its creation of development teams similar to IAVI's to step up the pace of AIDS vaccine research. The combined efforts of these and other groups of scientists may well meet the deadline set by President Clinton. But even if they do not, a real sense of urgency finally exists to find the vaccine or vaccines needed. And all concerned are certain that success is inevitable in the foreseeable future.

CHAPTER 6

Progress Toward Cancer Vaccines

A considerable amount of research is presently under way around the world to perfect effective cancer vaccines. At first glance, this may sound surprising, since cancer is not an infectious disease caused by invading germs, as are malaria, tuberculosis, influenza, and AIDS. No one "catches" cancer from inhaling germ-infested air or being bitten by a mosquito carrying a deadly microbe.

Instead, cancer consists of clusters of abnormal cells that appear and multiply within a person's body. With some exceptions (such as brain cells), most of the many different kinds of cells in the body divide now and then to produce fresh tissue. The cells that make up the skin are a clear example. About once a month, skin cells divide and the old cells fall away to make way for the new cells. Somehow, in ways scientists do not yet fully understand, the body signals normal cells that it is time to divide and also signals them when it is time to stop dividing.

In the case of cancer cells, by contrast, for some reason the signal to stop dividing does not get through, and the cells go on multiplying. They soon form a cluster, called a tumor, which more often than not grows larger and larger until it begins to press on nerves (causing pain) and nearby normal tissues. (Sometimes cells that do not get the signal to stop dividing multiply only very slowly and form tumors that prove harmless to the body. These tumors, referred to as benign, or "gentle," are not

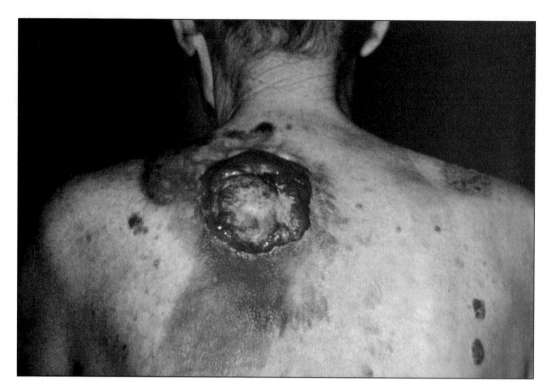

A malignant skin tumor, or solid mass of cancerous cells, on the back of a cancer patient.

cancerous; tumors composed of cancer cells are said to be malignant, or "harmful.") Cancerous cells not only grow into malignant tumors, but also invade normal, healthy cells, causing the disease to spread.

A cancerous growth that appears in one part of the body—the lung, for instance—may stay confined to that area, destroying more and more normal tissue until the person dies. Any part of the body can be affected in this way; in fact, more than two hundred different kinds of cancer are known, among them cancer of the skin, breast, brain, stomach, prostate gland, colon (part of the large intestine), and bones. (A few kinds of cancer do not form solid masses, but attack the cells in the body's fluids. Those that attack the blood, for example, are called leukemias.) Cancer cells from one part of the body frequently migrate and multiply in other areas. This deadly formation of new kinds of tumors is called metastasis, the occurrence of which significantly increases the likelihood that the patient will die.

In fact, cancer is an extremely debilitating and lethal disease that kills more than 6 million people worldwide a year. In the United States alone, about 2.3 million people are diagnosed with cancer each year and more than half a million die from it. The fact that some people who get cancer do *not* die from it is attributable to several factors. First, on occasion cancer can stop growing and spreading, or even shrink, all on its own, a process called remission. Most often, the increasing rate of survival among cancer sufferers is the result of aggressive medical treatments. The traditional ones include surgery (removing the cancerous tumor before it metastasizes); radiation (which bombards the cancerous cells, killing them); and chemotherapy (which employs powerful drugs to fight the cancer and limit its growth).

Though these treatments can be and often are effective and save many lives each year, the number of deaths from cancer is still huge, and the constant appearance of millions of new cases of cancer a year is alarming. That

A brain tumor removed during a biopsy. Surgery is one of the traditional ways of fighting cancer.

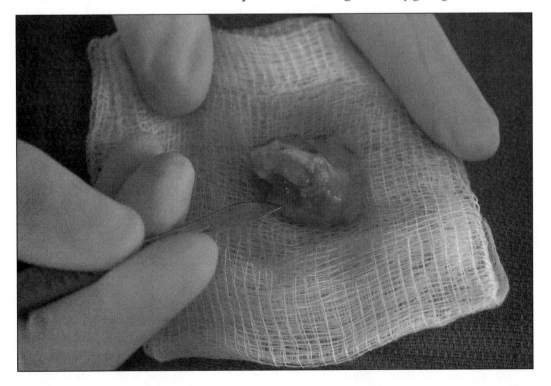

is why scientists feel that creating a cancer vaccine is so important. They believe that it is possible to find a substance (or substances) that will stimulate a person's immune system to attack and destroy cancer cells—in other words, a vaccine. An effective vaccine would not *prevent* cancer from growing in the first place, as the vaccines for polio prevent the onset of that disease in a healthy person. However, such a cancer vaccine would at least fight an existing cancer and eliminate the need for the traditional treatments, each of which can be, in and of itself, dangerous to the patient.

Pioneer of Cancer Vaccine Research

Although large-scale research into cancer vaccines is relatively new (having begun in earnest in the late 1970s), the idea of stimulating the immune system to fight cancer has been around for a long time. The major pioneer in the area was Dr. William B. Coley, a surgeon at Memorial Hospital in New York City. In the early 1890s, not long after he became a doctor, Coley and some colleagues noticed something strange in some of their patients who had cancerous tumors. When these patients acquired bacterial infections, especially near the tumors themselves, and fought off the infections, the tumors often got smaller. Coley realized that the infection had stimulated the immune system to fight it, and that various elements in that immune response had also attacked the tumor's cells, destroying enough of them to reduce the tumor's size.

Thereafter, Coley made it his life's work to develop therapies for cancer based on the body's immune response (which appropriately are called immunotherapies). He started by purposely injecting cancer patients with bacteria with the aim of causing an infection and stimulating the body's immune system. Sometimes he injected the bacteria right into the tumor itself. He eventually devised a killed bacterial vaccine he hoped would destroy cancerous tumors. In many cases, Coley's patients' tumors did shrink in size; but unfortunately, the results of his experiments varied widely from patient to patient and from one type of cancer to another. Because his treatments were unpredictable, and especially because scientists still did not understand fully how the body's immune response works, Coley's work did not come close to providing a cure for cancer.

Nonspecific Approaches

In hindsight, it is now clear that several factors were responsible for Coley's and other early researchers' lack of success. Besides the fact that they did not fully understand the workings of the immune system, they also approached the problem of immunotherapy for cancer in a "nonspecific" manner. Says noted modern cancer researcher Lloyd J. Old, "Coley's approach to cancer therapy . . . strengthened the overall activity of the immune system instead of selectively arousing those elements most able to combat cancer."[32] In other words, because Coley did not specifically target cancer, much less a *specific kind* of cancer, but instead only stimulated

A False Lead?

In the wake of William B. Coley's work (from the 1890s to early 1930s) on stimulating immune responses to attack cancer, other early cancer researchers tried to develop immune system-based therapies. But like Coley, they still did not fully understand the inner workings of the human immune system. This naturally resulted in a number of wrong assumptions and false leads. During the 1960s and early 1970s, for example, researchers Lewis Thomas, of New York University, and MacFarlane Burnett, of Hall Institute (in Melbourne, Australia), suggested a novel idea. They proposed that, in some unknown manner, the immune system normally "surveys" the body, seeking out and destroying emerging cancer cells. Only when this surveillance system fails, they said, does cancer manage to gain a firm foothold and grow into a tumor. Many scientists at first embraced this scenario and began searching for the surveillance mechanisms. However, more recent research suggests that the body does *not* seek out most forms of cancer, and most scientists now view Thomas's and MacFarlane's theory as largely flawed.

the immune system in a general way, his treatments were only marginally successful.

This does not mean that vaccines that use a nonspecific approach to cancer are useless. Some of the more recent research in the area has produced nonspecific vaccines that work in a limited way in certain situations. Old here describes one that kills the small numbers of cells of superficial bladder cancer that sometimes begin growing back in patients who have had bladder tumors removed. This cancer, he says,

> responds well to a vaccine called BCG, used to combat tuberculosis. These molecules do not cause disease because they evoke [stimulate] a strong immune response. Superficial bladder cancer typically recurs after surgery [in which a bladder tumor has been removed] and, in its later phases, invades the bladder wall and beyond. But instilling BCG into the bladder . . . elicits [produces] . . . a prolonged activation of immune cells that fight invaders. Just how the cells work is not understood in detail, but the end result is

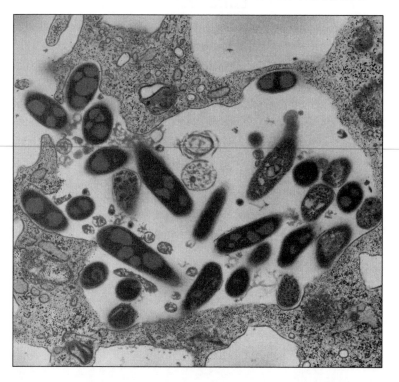

A BCG vaccine (the dark ovals) infects a human macrophage white blood cell. BCG vaccines may offer some protection against cancer.

that the immune cells and the substances they secrete [give off] kill preexisting and developing cancer cells in the bladder wall. Consequently, patients who receive BCG [after their operations] face a much lower risk of [the cancer returning].[33]

Thus, the BCG vaccine stimulates a general, nonspecific immune response in the bladder area, and the relatively small growths of cancerous bladder cells happen to be susceptible to this sudden influx of T cells, antibodies, and other disease-fighting agents. Unfortunately, most cancers remain unaffected by this sort of nonspecific immune response. Early cancer vaccine researchers would have benefited tremendously, therefore, by utilizing a more specific approach—one that singled out and attacked a specific cancer.

More Specific Approaches

Coley and the others were unable to employ such a specific strategy because of another limitation they faced. For the body's defensive cells to attack a specific type of tumor, those cells have to be able to recognize abnormal cells from normal cells, and also to mark the abnormal cells for death. In the early years of the twentieth century, scientists learned that antibodies, the special proteins manufactured by white blood cells, perform this task expertly. Antibodies can detect tiny distinctions among antigens and cells by recognizing specific molecules coating their outer surfaces. After the antibodies zero in on invading antigens and render them harmless, they mark their foes for destruction (by the large macrophages that then devour the invaders). At the same time, the antibodies can distinguish between such invaders and normal body cells, which also carry distinctive molecular "fingerprints."

It stood to reason that, like invading antigens and normal body cells, cancer cells would have their own distinctive fingerprints. (Scientists came to call these cancer-cell fingerprints "antigens," after the foreign-invader type of antigen.) But in the case of most kinds

A human breast cancer cell. The antigens of cancer cells are not detectable by antibodies.

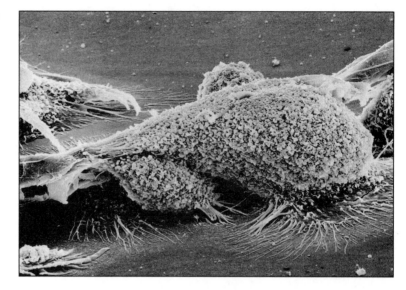

of cancer, these distinctive antigens were apparently invisible to the antibodies; this explained why a cancerous tumor could grow larger and larger without provoking an agressive attack by the immune system. If scientists could devise some way to make the antigens coating the cancer cells visible to the immune system, they could conceivably target a certain kind of cancer with a vaccine based on antibodies that recognized that specific cancer. The problem was where to get such specially programmed antibodies. The sad reality was that researchers lacked the technical means to produce large numbers of a specific kind of antibody, both for study and for use in a vaccine.

Medical science finally began to overcome that limitation in 1975 thanks to two scientists working at the University of Cambridge, in England. Cesar Milstein and Georges J. F. Kohler found a way to fuse (bring together as one) normal antibody-making cells with cancerous cells taken from a mouse. The result was cells that reproduced and grew into a mass, just as cancer cells do, but that also produced antibodies. Moreover, all of the cells in any discrete mass were clones of one another, and therefore identical; similarly, all of the antibodies they produced were of the same kind. For this reason, Milstein and Kohler, who received the Nobel Prize for their achievement, called them monoclonal ("one clone") antibodies.

Various Antibody Therapies

In retrospect, this "spectacular technology," as Old puts it, marked the real beginning of modern cancer vaccine research. But at the time, as has happened often with such major scientific breakthroughs, many researchers mistakenly thought the end of their quest—in this case, a successful cancer vaccine—was just around the corner. There were "premature and unrealistic assertions about antibodies as 'magic bullets,'" Old explains:

> It was hoped that monoclonal antibodies would home in on cancer cells . . . and trigger an immune attack that destroyed the target cells but ignored normal cells. . . . Many expected that these bullets could be made more deadly by loading them with toxic chemicals; the antibodies would carry the toxins directly to the tumors, where the poisons would kill cancer cells. Excitement prompted industry and private investors to spend vast sums of money. But when the claims could not be substantiated as quickly as everyone had hoped, opinion swung in the other direction, prompting many analysts and investors to declare that the technology had failed. The reality of the situation is far more positive. The concept remains sound, and slow, steady progress is being made in developing antibody therapies [for cancer].[34]

British molecular biologist Dr. Cesar Milstein, one of the developers of monoclonal antibodies.

In fact, so many ideas for and approaches to such antibody therapies for cancer have been suggested in recent years that too few labs and qualified researchers exist to test them all. Some of these follow traditional approaches, such as using the

A Careful, Laborious Process

Nonscientists often do not fully understand why it takes so long to develop a new vaccine, especially one for a disease as complex, diverse, and deadly as cancer. Consider as illustration an antibody cancer therapy that began development at the Memorial Sloan-Kettering Cancer Center, in New York City, in 1982. That was the year that researchers managed to identify an antigen that coats colon cancer cells. They did this by engineering a monoclonal antibody derived from mouse tissue. To prepare a vaccine for initial trials with animals required so many studies and laboratory experiments, six years passed before such trials could begin. The animals had to be monitored for many months and the results of these tests studied and evaluated for many more months. Then came the careful, laborious process of preparing a similar vaccine suitable for human subjects. This work continued until 1995. These tests, in their turn, had to be evaluated, and then repeated, each new test giving the researchers a fresh perspective on the work. That work continues today.

antibodies to target the antigens of specific cancer tumors. Injected into the cancerous area of a patient, such an "antigen vaccine" would hopefully stimulate the body to produce large numbers of killer T cells, which would zero in on and destroy the cancer cells bearing the targeted antigen. Another traditional approach is to rig the antibodies to carry toxic substances (including plant toxins and various radioactive compounds) directly to tumors.

A newer antibody cancer vaccine that shows promise involves engineering antibodies to attack the stroma, the tissue that connects one cancerous tumor cell to another. The stroma makes up as much as 60 percent of any cancerous mass; without it, a tumor cannot grow past microscopic size, in which case it remains harmless to the body. In the late 1990s, researchers at the Memorial Sloan-Kettering Cancer Center in New York City identified certain antigens that coat the stroma; this knowledge may well lead to a vaccine that directs the immune system to attack the stroma.

Dendritic Cells and DNA

Other innovative cancer vaccines presently under development use approaches that focus on other agents besides antibodies. One of these agents is a less-familiar soldier in the body's army of microscopic defenders—the dendritic cell. These cells, which regularly patrol the body, carry around tiny bits and pieces of harmful germs and use these pieces as markers to show other immune cells, such as the killer T cells, which invaders to attack. "To make a dendritic cell vaccine," science writer Kevin Bonsor explains,

> scientists extract some of the patient's dendritic cells and
> . . . reproduce large amounts of dendritic cells in the lab.
> These dendritic cells are then exposed to antigens [that
> have been extracted] from the patient's cancer cells. This
> combination of dendritic cells and antigens is then inject-
> ed into the patient, and the dendritic cells work to pro-
> gram the T-cells [with information identifying the specific
> cancer antigen involved].[35]

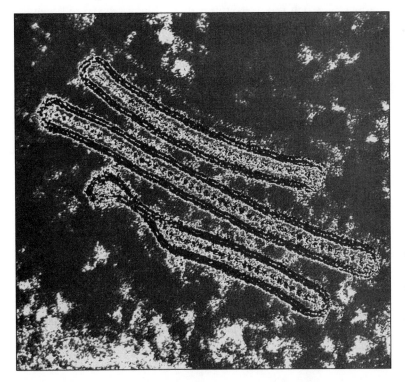

Three Birbeck granules in a human dendritic cell. Birbeck granules ingest antigens and excrete them in modified form, which the dendritic cells carry around to use in attacking invading antigens.

Scientists are also working on genetically engineered DNA vaccines to fight cancer. One of these uses a recombinant vehicle, in this case a virus. First, the researchers render the virus harmless. Then they manipulate the DNA of the virus, in a sense encoding it with the specific signature of the antigen coating the cancer cells they want to attack. When the researchers administer the virus to a patient, it enters the person's cells and influences those cells to produce antigens that look like those of the cancer. This in turn stimulates the immune system to produce larger-than-normal numbers of killer T cells to attack the cancer.

It is important to emphasize that these and the dozens of other cancer vaccines now in various stages of development are far from perfected. There still is no magic bullet, and the end of the quest is still not clearly in sight. "While scientists have had some success with each of [the many proposed] cancer vaccines," Bonsor points out in mid-2001,

> it is still much too early to predict when a true cancer vaccine will be developed. However, science has brought us closer than ever to being able to develop a method that could eradicate some forms of cancer in our lifetime, if not all cancer entirely.[36]

When that momentous day comes, people everywhere will once more invoke the names and honor the memo-

A Killed Cancer Vaccine

One present approach to developing cancer vaccines involves vaccinating patients with their own cancer cells. To make a so-called tumor-cell vaccine, researchers remove some cancer cells from the patient and kill them. Then they inject the dead cells back into the patient. Even though these cells are dead, they still have antigens on their outer surfaces, distinctive fingerprints that the immune system could conceivably recognize. Those working on such vaccines hope to stimulate the body to mount an immune response to attack the dead cells and that the T cells and other defensive agents in this response will also attack the live cancer cells in the tumor.

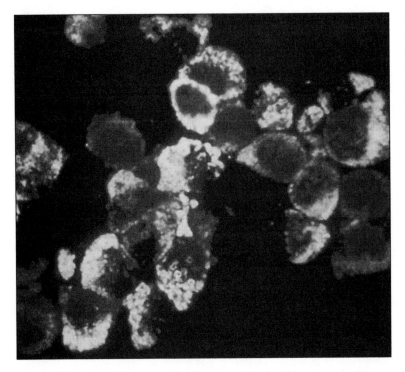

One of the many cancer vaccines in development. This one uses genetically engineered Vaccinia *viruses to target cervical cancer.*

ries of Jenner, Pasteur, Coley, and the other courageous and diligent medical pioneers who made life-saving vaccines possible. To such individuals, humanity owes, and surely will always owe, a debt so immense it can never be repaid.

NOTES

Chapter 1: Fighting Disease Before Vaccines

1. Quoted in *Modern History Sourcebook*, "Lady Mary Wortley Montagu: Smallpox Vaccination in Turkey," accessed May 6, 2001, p. 1 ,www.fordham.edu/halsall/mod/montagu-smallpox.html.
2. Quoted in "Lady Mary Wortley Montagu: Smallpox Vaccination in Turkey," p. 1.

Chapter 2: The Discovery of the First Vaccines

3. Quoted in A. J. Harding Rains, *Edward Jenner and Vaccination*. Hove, England: Wayland, 1974, p. 32.
4. Quoted in Rains, *Edward Jenner and Vaccination*, p. 36.
5. Quoted in Rains, *Edward Jenner and Vaccination*, p. 37.
6. Quoted in René Valery-Radot, *The Life of Pasteur*. Trans. R. L. Devonshire. Garden City, NY: Garden City, 1926, p. 120.
7. Quoted in Valery-Radot, *Life of Pasteur*, p. 124.
8. Quoted in Madeleine P. Grant, *Louis Pasteur: Fighting Hero of Science*. New York: McGraw-Hill, 1959, p. 66.
9. Quoted in Grant, *Louis Pasteur*, p. 67.
10. Quoted in Grant, *Louis Pasteur*, p. 68.
11. Quoted in Valery-Radot, *Life of Pasteur*, p. 142.

Chapter 3: Early Triumphs of Immunology

12. Quoted in Harold Faber and Doris Faber, *American Heroes of the 20th Century*. New York: Random House, 1967, p. 71.
13. Quoted in Faber and Faber, *American Heroes*, p. 72.

14. Quoted in Hugh G. Ghallager, *FDR's Splendid Deception: The Moving Story of Roosevelt's Massive Disability and the Intense Efforts to Conceal It from the Public.* New York: Dodd Mead, 1985, p. 23.

15. Quoted in Faber and Faber, *American Heroes*, p. 93.

16. Quoted in Faber and Faber, *American Heroes*, p. 98.

Chapter 4: New Horizons for Vaccines

17. Quoted in David Graham, "Scripps Seeks to Develop Vaccine to Combat Resurgence of Malaria," *San Diego Union-Tribune*, May 10, 1992, p. 2.

18. Anna Aldovini and Richard A. Young, "The New Vaccines," *Technology Review*, January 1992, p. 3.

19. David B. Weiner and Ronald C. Kennedy, "Genetic Vaccines," *Scientific American*, July 1999, p. 24.

20. W. H. Langridge, "Edible Vaccines," *Scientific American*, September 2000, p. 12.

21. Quoted in *Seedling*, "Eat Up Your Vaccines," December 2000, p. 2, www.grain.org/publications/dec00/dec001. htm.

Chapter 5: The Continuing Search for an AIDS Vaccine

22. Jon Cohen, *Shots in the Dark: The Wayward Search for an AIDS Vaccine.* New York: W. W. Norton, 2001, p. xvi.

23. Aldovini and Young, "The New Vaccines," p. 27.

24. Cohen, *Shots in the Dark*, p. 39.

25. Cohen, *Shots in the Dark*, p. 103.

26. Bill Clinton, "Commencement Address by the President of the United States at Morgan State University," May 18, 1997, www.aegis.com/hivinfoweb/library/vaccines/ goal9705.html.

27. "Nine Years and Counting: Will We Have an HIV Vaccine by 2007? An Agenda for Action for an HIV Vaccine," report published by the AIDS Vaccine Advocacy Coalition, May 1998, p. 5.

28. "Scientific Blueprint for AIDS Vaccine Development,"

report published by the International AIDS Vaccine Institute, June 1998, p. 2.

29. Meredith Wadman, "How Close Is the AIDS Vaccine?" *Fortune*, November 13, 2000, p. 13.

30. Wadman, "How Close Is the AIDS Vaccine?" p. 14.

31. *IRIN HIV/AIDS Weekly*, "Kenya: Researchers Vouch for Safety of AIDS Vaccine Trial," March 9, 2001, www.relief web.int/IRIN/hiv_aids/weekly/20010309.phtml.

Chapter 6: Progress Toward Cancer Vaccines

32. Lloyd J. Old, "Immunotherapy for Cancer," *Scientific American*, September 1996, p. 19.

33. Old, "Immunotherapy for Cancer," pp. 19–20.

34. Old, "Immunotherapy for Cancer," pp. 23—24.

35. Kevin Bonsor, "How Cancer Vaccines Will Work," *How Stuff Works*, accessed May 6, 2001, p. 3, www.howstuff works.com/cancer-vaccine.htm.

36. Bonsor, "How Cancer Vaccines Will Work," p. 3.

GLOSSARY

antibodies: Proteins manufactured by the body's white blood cells to defend against invading disease germs.

antigen: A harmful substance, usually part or all of a disease germ that invades the body.

antitoxin: A substance that neutralizes a toxin.

artificial immunity: Immunity imparted by injecting the body with a substance, such as a vaccine, that stimulates the immune system.

attenuation: The weakening of harmful disease germs for use in a vaccine.

booster shot: A follow-up vaccination to keep active the body's immunity to a certain disease.

contraceptive vaccine: A vaccine that prevents pregnancy.

culture: A laboratory growth of germs for medical study or use.

DNA and RNA: Deoxyribonucleic acid and ribonucleic acid; the major components of the genetic materials of living things.

DNA vaccine: A vaccine that uses DNA fragments from harmful germs to program human cells to create an immune response.

genetic engineering: Human manipulation of the genetic materials of living things.

genetics: The study of heredity (the transmission of physical characteristics from one generation to another).

germ theory: The concept that germs cause disease.

immune response: The body's defensive reaction to harmful substances that invade it from the outside.

immunity: The process by which the body resists disease.

immunology: The study of the process of immunity and the prevention of disease. A person who specializes in immunology is called an immunologist.

inoculation: The practice of injecting the body with a form of a disease to ward off future attacks of that disease.

killed vaccine: A vaccine made of germs that have been rendered harmless by killing them.

live vaccine: A vaccine made of living germs.

lymphocyte: A white blood cell that manufactures or aids in the manufacture of the body's defensive forces during an immune response.

macrophage: A large defensive body cell that destroys harmful germs.

monoclonal antibodies: Antibodies produced by special cells created by fusing antibody-producing cells with cancer cells. The special cells reproduce, each new copy a clone of and therefore identical to the others; the antibodies these cells create are all of a single type.

mutation: An offspring that is significantly different genetically and/or physically from its parents.

natural immunity: Immunity gained by contracting and surviving a disease.

plasmids: Tiny pieces of DNA taken from bacteria for use in DNA vaccines.

polysaccharide vaccine: A vaccine made of the carbohydrate-rich outer shell of a germ.

recombinant DNA: DNA that has been artificially prepared by combining DNA fragments from members of different species.

recombinant vehicle vaccine: A vaccine made of harmless germs that have been artificially altered to carry genetic information taken from harmful germs.

strain: A variation of a specific kind of disease germ.

stroma: The tissue that connects one cancer cell to another.

subunit vaccine: A vaccine made of disease antigens that have been artificially altered by being grown in cultures of harmless germs.

synthetic peptide vaccine: A vaccine made of artificial chemical copies of parts of microscopic parasites.

T cells: Short for *cytotoxic T lymphocytes;* these are special lymphocytes that can attack various foreign antigens, as well as virus-infected cells. Subtypes include killer T cells and helper T cells.

tolerance: The body's ability to withstand a disease.

toxin: A poison.

toxoid vaccine: A vaccine made of antitoxins.

vaccination: The process of administering a vaccine.

vaccine: A substance that provides protection against a specific disease by triggering the body's natural immune system without passing on the disease itself.

FOR FURTHER READING

Faith H. Brynie, *101 Questions About Your Immune System You Felt Defenseless to Answer . . . Until Now*. Brookfield, CT: Twenty-First Century Books, 2000. A well-organized, informative introduction to the body's immune system.

Ann Fullick, *Louis Pasteur*. Crystal Lake, IL: Heinemann Library, 2000. The life of the great scientist who helped prove the germ theory of disease and also developed the first attenuated vaccines is effectively covered in this readable biography.

Great Disasters: Dramatic Stories of Nature's Awesome Powers. Pleasantville, NY: Reader's Digest Association, 1989. A large, informative book that covers several historical disease epidemics, including some caused by smallpox.

Andrew T. McPhee, *AIDS*. Danbury, CT: Franklin Watts, 2000. McPhee explains the background and mortality rates of AIDS, as well as research into cures for the disease, in a straightforward manner.

Don Nardo, *Germs: Mysterious Microorganisms*. San Diego: Lucent Books, 1991. A general overview of the basic kinds of germs, how they cause disease, and how they are used today in numerous nonmedical ways, such as sewage treatment and oil spill cleanup.

Tom Ridgway, *Smallpox*. New York: Rosen, 2001. An up-to-date synopsis of the history of one of the worst diseases in history, with a detailed section on how Jenner developed the first vaccine.

Neil Shulman et al., *The Germ Patrol: All About Shots for Tots . . . and Big Kids, Too!* Decatur, GA: RX Humor, 1998. This clever volume introduces children to the basic reasons doctors give people shots, including vaccination and how it helps fight germs.

MAJOR WORKS CONSULTED

Books

Jon Cohen, *Shots in the Dark: The Wayward Search for an AIDS Vaccine*. New York: W. W. Norton, 2001. Cohen, a noted science writer who has tackled a number of controversial topics, including cloning, here delivers a frank, extremely well researched exposé on the reasons, some technical, others political and financial, why scientists have not yet been able to produce an effective AIDS vaccine. He also outlines newer, more hopeful initiatives to find such a vaccine in the near future. Highly recommended.

E. A. M. Jacob, *Louis Pasteur: Hunting Killer Germs*. New York: McGraw-Hill, 2000. A fine, up-to-date biography of one of the greatest scientists who ever lived, with plenty of information about Pasteur's work on vaccines.

Andrew Morgan et al., *The Eradication of Smallpox: Edward Jenner and the First and Only Eradication of an Infectious Disease*. San Diego: Academic Press, 2000. One of the better recent books about past medical figures, this one not only effectively covers Jenner and the discovery of the first vaccine, but also follows up with the story of how twentieth-century researchers finally made a concerted effort to wipe out smallpox and succeeded.

William A. Muraskin, *The Politics of International Health: The Children's Vaccine Institute and the Struggle to Develop*

Vaccines for the Third World. Albany: State University of New York Press, 1998. Explains about efforts to provide vaccines for people in poorer countries, where many nonmedical problems, including lack of education and local corruption, play roles in keeping sick people from getting the medicine they need.

Paul Offit, *What Every Parent Needs to Know About Vaccines*. New York: Macmillan, 1998. In addition to explaining how vaccines work, Offit tries to explain the positions of both sides in the current debate (mainly in nonmedical circles) about whether or not vaccines are safe and effective. He does, however, ultimately side with most doctors in concluding that vaccines are mainly (although not 100 percent) safe.

Nina G. Seavey et al., *A Paralyzing Fear: The Triumph over Polio in America*. New York: TV Books, 1998. A well-written, fact-filled overview of how Salk, Sabin, and other researchers developed vaccines to conquer polio, which once crippled hundreds of thousands of people, most of them children.

Jacqueline Sharon, *Basic Immunology*. Baltimore: Wilkins and Wilkins, 1998. This recent textbook, which explains the workings of the immune system in considerable detail (and also explains how vaccines stimulate an immune response) will appeal mainly to scholars and medical students.

René Valery-Radot, *The Life of Pasteur*. Trans. R . L. Devonshire. Garden City, NY: Garden City, 1926. Though many more recent biographies of Pasteur are available, this work remains valuable for its many primary source quotations taken from books, newspapers, and other documents of Pasteur's day.

Periodicals and Reports

Anna Aldovini and Richard A. Young, "The New Vaccines," *Technology Review*, January 1992.

Elizabeth M. Jaffe, "Progress Toward Cancer Vaccines," *Hospital Practice*, December 15, 2000.

W. H. Langridge, "Edible Vaccines," *Scientific American*, September 2000.

"Nine Years and Counting: Will We Have an HIV Vaccine by 2007? An Agenda for Action for an HIV Vaccine," report published by the AIDS Vaccine Advocacy Coalition, May 1998.

Lloyd J. Old, "Immunotherapy for Cancer," *Scientific American*, September 1996.

Meredith Wadman, "How Close Is the AIDS Vaccine?" *Fortune*, November 13, 2000.

David B. Weiner and Ronald C. Kennedy, "Genetic Vaccines," *Scientific American*, July 1999.

Internet Sources

Alfred E. Chang, "Cancer Vaccines: A Primer About an Emerging Therapy," *CancerNews*, January 2000, www.cancernews.com/vaccines.

Bill Clinton, "Commencement Address by the President of the United States at Morgan State University," May 18, 1997, www.aegis.com/hivinfoweb/library/vaccines/goal9705.html.

P. D. Griffin, "Contraceptive Vaccines," *World Health Organization*, accessed May 14, 2001, http://matweb.hcuge.ch/matweb/endo/Reproductive_health/Contraceptives_vaccines.html.

R. Paul Johnson and Spyros Kalams, "The Science of HIV Vaccine Development," *HIV InSite Knowledge Base Chapter*, May 1998, www.thebody.com/trat/vaccines.html.

ADDITIONAL WORKS CONSULTED

Books

Keith A. Crandall, ed., *The Evolution of HIV*. Baltimore: Johns Hopkins University Press, 1999.

Edward Edelson, *The Immune System*. New York: Chelsea House, 1989.

Harold Faber and Doris Faber, *American Heroes of the 20th Century*. New York: Random House, 1967.

Hugh G. Ghallager, *FDR's Splendid Deception: The Moving Story of Roosevelt's Massive Disability and the Intense Efforts to Conceal It from the Public*. New York: Dodd Mead, 1985.

Henry G. Grabowski, *The Search for New Vaccines: The Effects of the Vaccines for Children Program*. Washington, DC: AEI Press, 1997.

Madeleine P. Grant, *Louis Pasteur: Fighting Hero of Science*. New York: McGraw-Hill, 1959.

Sharon G. Humiston and Cynthia Good, *Vaccinating Your Child: Questions and Answers for the Concerned Parent*. Atlanta: Peachtree Publishers, 2000.

A. J. Harding Rains, *Edward Jenner and Vaccination*. Hove, England: Wayland, 1974.

Neil Z. Miller, *Immunization: The People Speak*. Santa Fe: New Atlantean Press, 1996.

B. R. Murphy and R. M. Chanock, *Immunization Against Virus Disease*. Philadelphia: Lippincott-Raven, 1996.

Stanley A. Plotkin et al., eds., *Vaccines*. St. Louis: W. B. Saunders, 1999.

Marianne Tully and Mary-Alice Tully, *Dread Diseases*. New York: Franklin Watts, 1978.

George F. Vande Woude and George Klein, eds., *Advances in Cancer Research*. San Diego: Academic Press, 1999.

Bruce A. Voyles, *The Biology of Viruses*. New York: McGraw-Hill, 1993.

Periodicals and Reports

David Graham, "Scripps Seeks to Develop Vaccine to Combat Resurgence of Malaria," *San Diego Union-Tribune*, May 10, 1992.

B. F. Haynes, "HIV Vaccines: Where We Are and Where We Are Going," *Lancet*, vol. 348, 1996.

"Intensifying Action Against HIV/AIDS in Africa: Responding to a Development Crisis," report published by the World Bank, June 1999.

D. W. Kufe, "Smallpox, Polio and Now a Cancer Vaccine?" *Nature Medicine*, March 6, 2000.

"Report on the Global HIV/AIDS Epidemic," published by Joint United Nations Programme on HIV/AIDS, June 2000.

"Scientific Blueprint for AIDS Vaccine Development," report published by the International AIDS Vaccine Institute, June 1998.

J. Travis, "Fused Cells Hold Promise of Cancer Vaccines," *Science News*, March 4, 2000.

Internet Sources

AIDS Treatment News, "First HIV Vaccine for Africa Begins Trials," January 26, 2001, www.thebody.com/treat/vaccines.html.

Kevin Bonsor, "How Cancer Vaccines Will Work," *How Stuff Works*, accessed May 6, 2001, www.howstuffworks.com/cancer-vaccine.htm.

A. G. Dalgleish, "Cancer Vaccines and Gene Therapy: Current Clinical Trials," St. George's Hospital Medical

School, n.d., www.tustison.com/dal.htm.

French Press Agency, "Kenya—AIDS Vaccine: Clinical Trial of AIDS Vaccine Under Way in Kenya," March 6, 2001, www.aegis.com/news/afp/2001AF010326.html.

IRIN HIV/AIDS Weekly, "Kenya: Researchers Vouch for Safety of AIDS Vaccine Trial," March 9, 2001, www.reliefweb.int/IRIN/hiv_aids/weekly/20010309.phtml.

Medscape and Prometheus Books, Edward R. Friedlander, "Opposition to Immunization: A Pattern of Deception," 2001, accessed May 6, 2001, www.medscape.com/prometheus/SRAM/2001/v05.n01/sram0501.03.fried/-sram0501.03.fried01.html.

Modern History Sourcebook, "Lady Mary Wortley Montagu: Smallpox Vaccination in Turkey," accessed May 6, 2001, www.fordham.edu/halsall/mod/montagu-smallpox.html.

National Institute of Allergy and Infectious Diseases, "HIV Vaccine Glossary," May 2000. www.thebody.com/treat/vaccines.html.

David Olle, "Cancer Vaccines," January 23, 2001, www.suite101.com/article.cfm/9718/57009.

Pickering Women's Classics, "Turkish Embassy Letters by Lady Mary Wortley Montagu," accessed May 11, 2001, www.pickeringchatto.com/turkishembassy.htm.

Seedling, "Eat Up Your Vaccines," December 2000, www.grain.org/publications/dec00/dec001.htm.

INDEX

PICTURE CREDITS

Cover photo: © David Kelly Crow/PhotoEdit/PictureQuest
© AFP/CORBIS, 68
© Lester V. Bergman/CORBIS, 96
© Bettmann/CORBIS, 103
© Biophoto Associates/Photo Researchers, Inc., 102
Tim Boyle/Newsmakers/Liaison, 65
John Chiasson/Liaison, 84
© Russell D. Curtis/Photo Researchers, Inc., 71
Dr. Brian Eyden/Science Photo Library/Photo Researchers, Inc., 105
Hulton/Archive by Getty Images, 22, 25, 39, 42, 55
Fanie Jason/Liaison, 81
Johns Hopkins Medical Institutions/Science Photo Library/Photo
    Researchers, Inc., 107
Library of Congress, 31, 36, 37, 56, 89
London School of Hygiene & Tropical Medicine/Science Photo
    Library/Photo Researchers, Inc., 17
© Wally McNamee/CORBIS, 86
National Archives, 58, 61, 62
National Library of Medicine, 10, 15, 21, 29, 32, 47, 54, 67
National Library of Medicine/UNRQA/WHO photo by George
    Nehmeh, 12
National Library of Medicine/WHO photo, 11, 19
NIBSC/Science Photo Library/Photo Researchers, Inc., 100
North Wind Picture Archives, 20, 24, 45
Michael J. Okoniewski/Newsmakers/Liaison, 76, 78
PhotoDisc, 70
© Roger Ressmeyer/CORBIS, 97
© Reuters NewMedia Inc./CORBIS, 92
Martha Schierholz, 49, 50
Science Photo Library/Photo Researchers, Inc., 41, 73
Sinclair Stammers/Science Photo Library/Photo Researchers, Inc., 91

ABOUT THE AUTHOR

In addition to his numerous acclaimed volumes on ancient civilizations, historian Don Nardo has published several studies of modern scientific discoveries and phenomena. Among these are *The Extinction of the Dinosaurs, Cloning,* and a biography of Charles Darwin. Mr. Nardo lives with his wife, Christine, in Massachusetts.